Words of Life

THE BIBLE DAY BY DAY

SEPTEMBER–DECEMBER 2008

HODDER

Copyright © 2008 by The Salvation Army
International Headquarters, 101 Queen Victoria Street,
London EC4V 4EH

First published in Great Britain in 2008

1

British Library Cataloguing in Publication Data
A record for this book is available from the British Library

ISBN 978 0340 94380 9

Printed and bound in Great Britain by
Clays Ltd, St Ives plc

The paper and board used in this paperback are natural recyclable
products made from wood grown in sustainable forests.
The manufacturing processes conform to the environmental
regulations of the country of origin.

Hodder & Stoughton
A Division of Hodder Headline Ltd
338 Euston Road
London NW1 3BH
www.hodderfaith.com

Contents

SUNDAYS

In keeping with the custom of *Words of Life* to treat Sunday readings differently from those for the other days of the week, most of the Sunday readings in this edition feature songs and prayer-poems by the author, in which brevity and poetry combine powerfully to crystallise great truths in a few words.

From the Writer of *Words of Life* . . .

This volume of *Words of Life* is the final one from my keyboard. It has been a privilege to follow in the footsteps of the dozen men and women who, over half a century, have interpreted age-old Scripture for contemporary generations, and in tribute to them I have included extracts from four such writers – Majors Fred Brown, Clifford Kew and David Dalziel, and Commissioner Harry Read.

I have chosen extracts from their contributions for 1962, 1980, 1988 and 1999, which focus on the First Letter of Peter, the prophet Micah, the book of Proverbs and the disciples Judas Iscariot and James. Also included is a valued contribution from a present-day guest writer, Major James Bryden, who offers a helpful study on Paul's letter to the Ephesians.

From my own heart and mind, to begin this book, come thoughts which reflect the sad fact that warfare is an ever-present reality for planet Earth. And so I begin by considering how the military success and failure of the Israelites was closely linked to their trust in, and obedience to, God. There are present-day lessons to be learned here, particularly from the military leader Gideon.

As has been usual over the past two years, I am also responsible for the Sunday readings, most of which feature prayer-poems and songs from my pen, in which I try to crystallise great truths in a few words. Finally, I close the book with thoughts which take us up to Christmas and on to the close of the year.

So, farewell, readers! And welcome to my successor, Major Evelyn Merriam, who from the bustling American city of New York will continue to enable *Words of Life* readers around the world to hear the voice of God afresh – with a North American accent!

John Gowans
General (Retired)

Abbreviations

Gideon – God's Man for the Moment

Introduction

In these early years of the twenty-first century most of us have had quite enough of war. Older readers will recall living through a world war that saw the death of tens of millions of people, including millions who took no part in the fighting but sacrificed their lives nonetheless. Only the very young will have no memories of the 'cold war' between East and West, and all of us now have to face the constant fear of terrorist atrocities.

We could be forgiven, therefore, for finding the prospect of being soldiers of God a less appealing metaphor than once it was. It's there in Scripture, however, along with examples of men and women who fought bravely for God, both literally and figuratively. Gideon was one such – a brave military leader who demonstrated courage and resourcefulness in the divine cause. There is much we can learn from him – even if we are the 'quiet' men and women who win battles strategically, in the manner of chess masters rather than generals.

> I'm not a man of peace
> And quite calm.
> My fingers itch
> To sound out the alarm,
> To call to battle,
> Mobilise the good,
> And storm the forts of darkness!
> Understood?
>
> But I can see, O Lord,
> That now and then
> Great battles have been won
> By quiet men,
> Who bring a sense of peace
> And priestly poise;
> And no noise!

Listen and Learn

'The Israelites did evil in the eyes of the LORD, and for seven years he gave them into the hands of the Midianites' (v. 1).

The Israelites saw the strength of the Midianites, reinforced by their allies, and capitulated to them. It resulted in the Israelites suffering poverty and shame, hiding in caves. The invaders 'did not spare a living thing for Israel, neither sheep nor cattle nor donkeys' (v. 4). The Israelites' problem was that, having turned to other gods, they were too proud to seek help from their true God. It was a tragic situation, eventually so serious that the Israelites did at last cry out to the Lord for help. In response, God sent them Gideon.

God's children – in both Old and New Testament times – have always needed to listen and learn from the men and women God sends to them with words from himself. Sometimes those words are a call to arms, for evil is not destroyed accidentally or without effort. It was George Bernard Shaw who, a hundred and more years ago, declared in his play *Major Barbara*: 'It is a very significant thing, this instinctive choice of the military form of organisation, this substitution of the drum for the organ, by The Salvation Army. Does it not suggest that the Salvationists divine that they must actually fight the devil instead of merely praying at him?'

Victory always comes at a cost. It is a dangerous temptation for individual Christians, whole congregations or the Church at large to think evil can be managed without the Christ. When we begin to believe we can handle our temptations we are on the road to disaster.

Yield not to temptation, for yielding is sin;
Each victory will help you some other to win.
Fight manfully onward, dark passions subdue;
Look ever to Jesus, he will carry you through.
Ask the Saviour to help you,
Comfort, strengthen and keep you;
He is willing to aid you,
He will carry you through.

Horatio Richmond Palmer

Called and Equipped

'When the angel of the LORD appeared to Gideon, he said,
"The LORD is with you, mighty warrior"' (v. 12).

Scripture reveals that the Almighty's plan often involves men and women – prophets, angels – passing on his wishes and commands to the people who belong to him . . . and also to those who have yet to discover that they belong to him too. Such prophets might be selected to serve in that capacity for life or just for a particular length of time or a single occasion. They include spiritual giants such as Abraham, Moses and Joshua. For a mighty battle against evil God called to his side a mighty warrior and equipped him for the task: Gideon – God's chosen man for the moment.

It was not unusual, in Old Testament history, for such a person to tremble in anticipation of the task ahead. The challenge had to be accepted in spite of fears and limited capacities. God assured Gideon that he would not face his enemies alone, declaring: 'Go in the strength you have . . . Am I not sending you?' (v. 14).

All Christians, new or mature, are called sooner or later to face up to evil. When that happens, we discover we have strength and stamina we never guessed we had, either within us or on call from the God we serve. We should never shrink from the task God gives us just because we don't feel up to it at the moment of commissioning. Through prayer we can connect with a God who will never abandon us, even if we think he has.

I find Gideon an attractive person and an honest one, humble enough to say to his Lord: 'My clan is the weakest in Manasseh, and I am the least in my family' (v. 15). It's good that we acknowledge our weakness, so long as we recognise God's strength on offer to us. The Lord's reply? 'I will be with you . . . Peace! Do not be afraid. You are not going to die' (vv. 16, 23).

God is your wisdom, God is your might,
God's ever near you, guiding aright;
He understands you, knows all you need;
Trusting in him you'll surely succeed.
Lucy Milward Booth-Hellberg[1]

Obeying Orders

••

'The LORD said to him [Gideon], "Peace! Do not be afraid.
You are not going to die." So Gideon built an altar to the LORD
there and called it The LORD is Peace' (vv. 23, 24).

Gideon was human enough to be afraid. But he was not the sort of man to allow his fears to dictate his decisions. He must have trembled when the Lord gave him seemingly audacious instructions. The evil worship of Baal was to end and the altar of Baal must be demolished. Gideon knew God was testing him, for the altar in question had been built by his own father, Joash.

Gideon's instructions continued: once that altar was demolished, a new altar was to be erected. 'Build a proper kind of altar to the LORD your God on the top of this height,' said God (v. 26). Gideon would have recognised that the instructions echoed those of God to Moses, recorded for us in Exodus 20:22-26. Gideon obeyed his orders.

What should we learn from the courage of Gideon? Evil has to be faced unequivocally. But we might note that Gideon took the strategic decision to carry out his orders during the hours of darkness. Courage, even in the Lord's name, doesn't always have to be reckless! Nor is initiative frowned upon. Jesus said his followers should be not just 'as innocent as doves' but 'as shrewd as snakes' (Matthew 10:16). Our Lord would surely have approved of Gideon's tactics.

An old Salvation Army song by pioneer officer Richard Slater doesn't shrink from the possibility that life will not always be easy. It offers good advice:

> When the road we tread is rough,
> Let us bear in mind,
> In our Saviour strength enough
> We may always find;
> Though the fighting may be tough
> Let our motto be:
> Go on, go on to victory![2]

The Signs are There

'Now all the Midianites, Amalekites and other eastern
peoples joined forces and crossed over the Jordan and camped
in the Valley of Jezreel' (v. 33).

The Old Testament system by which nations banded together temporarily in a common cause was not as efficient as happens today. No joint training, previously agreed tactics, or even mutually agreed objectives. Gideon had to bind together several armies with varied aims in mind, and he knew his non-Israelite allies had their own interests at heart. To say they were unreliable would be an understatement.

Read Judges 5:13–18 to understand some of the problems. Verse 16 poses a question to some of the troops: 'Why did you stay among the campfires to hear the whistling for the flocks?' The next verse asks: 'And Dan, why did he linger by the ships?' and tells us: 'Asher remained on the coast and stayed in his coves.' We might wonder, 'With such friends, who needs enemies?' No wonder Gideon wanted to be assured that God would be alongside him.

All Christians should be militant, both unitedly in our joint campaigns and individually in our personal struggles against evil. But just as we encourage each other in battle, so we should comfort and reassure each other when necessary. And that will be often.

Gideon needed such reassurance, and asked for it from the Lord. 'Give me a sign,' he pleaded (6:17). God gave him the sign he requested. Some time later, Gideon asked for another sign: 'If you will save Israel . . . look, I will place a wool fleece on the threshing-floor. If there is dew only on the fleece and all the ground is dry, then I will know' (vv. 36, 37). God did as he was asked. But still Gideon was not fully convinced. He said to God: 'Do not be angry with me. Let me make just one more request. Allow me one more test' (v. 39). Again, God complied. Gideon was given the reassurance he so desperately needed.

Let's not be too critical of Gideon's hesitance. I have been preaching the gospel for more than fifty years and I have never yet mounted the pulpit without inwardly admitting to God my need for inner reinforcement. Like Gideon, my prayers have always been answered. We really should believe it: all the promises of God are sure!

5

Too Many

∙∙∙

'The LORD said to Gideon, "You have too many men for
me to deliver Midian into their hands"' (v. 2).

The methods of the Almighty make us wonder sometimes. All we can do on occasion is take a deep breath and trust him. What sort of commander would demand a smaller army to lead into battle? But the truth is, one soldier plus God is ultimately greater than a multitude without him. The author of Psalm 20:6, 7 puts it well: 'Now I know that the LORD saves his anointed . . . Some trust in chariots and some in horses, but we trust in the name of the LORD our God.'

A church's material resources and personnel have their place, but its members should not rely on these things for success in their divine mission. What's important is the presence and power of God in their midst. And a large congregation is rarely more effective than a small one. An individual who has no appetite for the fight against evil is more of a burden than an asset.

The Lord said to Gideon that those of his soldiers lacking courage should go home. As a result Gideon's army of 22,000 became a smaller one of 10,000, and then a tiny one of just 300. However, 300 totally focused and completely dedicated warriors is to be prized, not bemoaned – even if its enemies are 'thick as locusts. Their camels could no more be counted than the sand on the seashore' (Judges 7:12).

And what happened next? Read the story – it's as exciting as an airport thriller! The result? Victory for God's army. Of course! Let's take note . . . and take heart!

∙∙∙

To ponder:
In one of his songs William Pearson (1832–92) encouraged early-day Salvationists: 'Fierce is the battle, but victory will come.'

For the Lord and for Gideon

....

'The three companies blew the trumpets and smashed the jars.
Grasping the torches in their left hands and holding in their right
hands the trumpets they were to blow, they shouted, "A sword
for the LORD and for Gideon!"' (v. 20).

You have to admit that torches and trumpets and earthenware jars are an unusual recipe for military success. And the addition of a catchy slogan – 'A sword for the LORD and for Gideon' – doesn't immediately add much. But success there was. Total, overwhelming victory. Gideon's tactics worked. Except, of course, it was the involvement of the Lord that did it.

The war cry which invoked the names of both Gideon and the Lord was not Gideon generously sharing the glory with God, but a declaration of the fact that the battle was conducted in God's name. It's just a shame that the slaughter which followed Gideon's victory reflected the ways of the world at that time, rather than our present-day understanding of the loving, forgiving, gracious God we serve.

We need to understand that the Israelites believed wiping out the enemy would please God. Nowadays we know differently. Someone has said that the best way of defeating your enemy is to make him your friend. There's truth in that, so long as it does not involve compromising vital principles. But seeking peaceful methods of resolving conflict is a very recent development. It was not practised much during the centuries we label BC.

Gideon's victory made him hugely popular among the Israelites. 'Rule over us . . . you have saved us,' they said (8:22). But Gideon knew where the glory lay, and who should govern the people of God. 'I will not rule over you . . . The LORD will rule over you,' he declared (8:23). Wise man! The result was to be forty years of peace.

....

To ponder:
'If the human race wishes to have a prolonged and indefinite period of material prosperity, they have only got to behave in a peaceful and helpful way toward one another.'
Sir Winston Churchill

Victory Over Temptation

....

'For forty days he was tempted by the devil' (v. 2).

Any Christian who is reluctant to admit to being tempted lest it reflects badly on his or her spirituality must reject the biblical account of Christ's forty days in the wilderness. The fact is, if the devil feels no need to tempt you, it is a sign not of your strength but of your ineffectiveness as a Christian. You are no threat to him and can safely be left alone. Christ was tempted, but was victorious through the grace of God. That same grace is available to each of us, and the same victory too.

Enemy

I hardly like
To talk about him;
Just to hear his name
Is quite enough
To bring to mind
The everlasting flame!
He takes the lovely thing
And twists
Its beauty to his will.
Distorts the very
Word of God
His purpose to fulfil.
The devil,
That's his name,
Persists.
No matter what I do.
He just will not
Leave me alone.
But then,
No more will you!

God's Secret Plan

Everything in heaven and earth shall find its fulfilment in Christ!

Introduction

*O*ur guest writer for the next three weeks is Major James Bryden. As a
young teenager and a non-churchgoer, James had a Damascus Road
encounter with Christ which was to lead to him joining The Salvation
Army. He was commissioned an officer in 1968 and, with his wife Helen,
has served in Scotland, South America, Zimbabwe and England.

Currently The Salvation Army's Territorial Ecumenical Officer for the
United Kingdom and Republic of Ireland, James is honoured to preach
God's Word in a variety of locations. He holds a Bachelor of Divinity degree
(Glasgow) and a Masters in systematic theology from King's College
London.

Prepare to climb the heights and walk in heavenly places! Enter
Ephesians in the power of the Spirit and discover where heaven and
earth meet. The mystery of God's eternal will and long-range plan is
out in the open. Everything in deepest heaven and planet Earth is to
be brought together 'under one head, even Christ'.

The letter to the Ephesians, written by the apostle Paul, is in a class
all of its own and is adorned by such accolades as 'the queen of the
Epistles' and 'the crown and climax of Pauline theology'. At its heart is
God's grace, lavished upon us through Christ.

The letter celebrates in prayer and praise that we, without hope and
far from God, are made *alive in Christ* and one with each other.
Through him our minds and hearts are enlightened and empowered by
his resurrection so that we, even we, radiate his darkness-shattering
light.

The transformed life of the believer is shown in personal integrity at
home and community; promotes purity and peace; and fights
fearlessly against social and spiritual injustice.

*For the Sunday readings, John Gowans continues to provide a prayer-poem
with a selected Bible passage.*

Credentials and Challenge

....

*'I, Paul am under God's plan as an apostle, a special agent of
Christ Jesus . . . to you faithful Christians at Ephesus. I greet you with
grace and peace' (vv. 1, 2, MSG).*

When you send a letter, email or text to a friend you want them to
know it's come from you. Writing to a stranger, you would need
to say a little more about yourself. Here Paul introduces himself,
addresses the readers, then adds a special greeting. No personal profile.
No hint of exceptional intellect. No reference to special status as a
leading figure in the Church of his day. Rather, Paul identifies with all
who possess God's gift of grace and peace.

He does, however, declare God-given credentials. As an apostle he's
been selected and sent at God's command in the service of Christ
Jesus. If you like, he had no say in the matter. God wanted it and that
was that.

The people of God are the 'saints' (v. 1), or 'faithful Christians'. Not
that they're perfect but, like Paul, they've been called out by God and
set apart for his special purpose. They are in the world physically, but
spiritually they are above it 'in Christ Jesus'. As Christians we live in
two places at the same time! While we are touched by our culture
where the African dances praise to God, the Americans mix patriotism
with faith and the British love pageantry and ceremony, as Christians
we are defined by Christ.

Today our lives are invaded by secularism and materialism. Political
correctness floods and undermines foundational truth. The Christian's
faith wrestles with rival takes on life. It's not clear what we can run
with and what we can't. Does it have to be this way? No. God's will for
us is to be *part of Christ* (John 15:1ff.) and *in Christ* (Colossians 3:1-3)
and to share his grace and peace with all.

....

Christ of Glory, Prince of Peace,
Let thy life in mine increase;
Though I live may it be shown
'Tis thy life and not my own.
Dwell within, that men may see
Christ, the living Christ, in me.
Colin Fairclough[3]

A Blest and Glorious Life

•••

*'And he made known to us the mystery of his will . . . to bring
all things in heaven and on earth together under one head,
even Christ' (vv. 9, 10).*

In these verses we prepare to climb the heights and walk in heavenly
places! We don't arrive at our destination because *we* planned the
route. God alone has made it happen. On arrival, mystery clears like
morning mist to reveal the glory of God's eternal plan for all people.
Before planets or people existed, God was 'busy devising a way to draw
us home to himself so that we may live with him and for him'⁴. He does
this through his Son, and by his Spirit he brings us into Christ.

Paul is on a roll of praise. He's so bowled over by the God of glory he
doesn't stop for breath. In the Greek, the passage consists of one
sentence. It's a prayer; it's a hymn of praise to God, and little wonder!
God has opened his home to us. Our name is on the door. We're his
adopted sons and daughters. He's lavished his love on us at great cost:
his only Son's 'blood poured out on the . . . Cross' (v. 7, *MSG*). Why? To
destroy sin, save us and make us one with him. We are now on the
receiving end of blessing on blessing on blessing! And all because of
God's grace.

What is so amazing about grace is not that God gives us *something*,
rather, it is God giving us *himself!* It's the sheer scale of our salvation
and the call to live for God in the world that takes your breath away.
The fact that God has made known the mystery of his will which is to
bring all things together in Christ is utterly staggering to the apostle. In
Christ we're God's chosen family, forgiven sinners. God has singled us
out for the special attention of the Holy Spirit. What we have now is
awesome; what we will have in glory is beyond words.

There's no holding back the swelling chorus of praise to our God!

••

To ponder:
God has lavished his love on us. Lord, how we love you!

Prayer and Power

....

*'I keep asking that . . . the glorious Father, may give you the
Spirit . . . so that you may know him better' (v. 17).*

The incredible work of the Spirit seen in the level of love and
practical commitment between the believers sends Paul's prayer
rocketing. He can't stop thanking God for them. He burns with a
powerful longing that God's Spirit will enable them to know Christ
deeply in mind and heart – an intelligent, practical and spiritual grasp
rolled into one; for the Spirit to open their eyes to see their God-calling,
hope and promise in Christ.

The whole experience is immense and glorious for the believer, and
little wonder! God himself is behind it all. His own almighty power that
raised Christ from the dead is the *same* power at work in all who trust
him.

This awesome power of God has been placed in Christ so that he is
'far above all rule and authority, power and dominion . . . and God
[has] placed all things under his feet' (vv. 21, 22). Whatever we might
think about the state of our world – its corrupt regimes, the atrocities
against humanity, the spread of drug culture, the abuse of women and
children – God is sovereign. 'God has placed everything under the
power of Christ' (v. 22, *JBP*). This means what it says, *everything*.
Governments, authorities, powers: none have supremacy. All are
answerable to Christ. He alone is in charge of all peoples and places
(Colossians 1:15–20). He is without rival or equal.

We live in a fallen and a free world at the same time. God did not
create robots but human beings. If there's any programming going on,
it's learned behaviour. If things are good or bad, it's mostly because of
free choices. Yes, God took a risk in making us as we are. He also provides an incredible life-changing power that can save and recreate us
in his Son, Jesus Christ. He will not force his will on us. He allows us
choice.

Christ also is in charge of the Church. The community of believers
in all its rich variety should add to its richness. Not always 'all one body
we', but at last it's pouring the oil of healing on wounds of rivalry and
opening doors to respect and reconciliation. The only way forward is
to know Christ better.

Dead or Alive?

....

'Though we were dead in our sins God, who is rich in mercy, because of the great love he had for us, gave us life together with Christ . . . by grace and not by achievement . . . you are saved' (vv. 4–6, JBP).

Here we have a micro-chip of Paul's theology on salvation. Clear, simple and profound. In ten verses (just one, in the Greek!) he brilliantly encapsulates the devastating consequences of the sinful life, what God has done about it and the response believers need to make.

The first three verses sketch a bleak picture. Because of sin, humans are the 'living dead', subject to a world that ignores God. They're enslaved to the 'ruler of the . . . air', to themselves, the 'present evil age' the 'pattern of the world' and, at times, Satan (see Galatians 1:4; Romans 12:2).

When I was young The Salvation Army labelled it 'worldliness'. It's still around. Why are Nazism and anti-Semitism on the rise? How do sexual relations become so distorted? Why is there just beneath the skin of so many a bottled-up rage, about to explode? Answer: people are bound to themselves, they are 'gratifying the cravings of [the] sinful nature' (v. 3) and alienated from God.

The only way to turn things around is for God to enter the picture and do for humanity what it cannot do for itself. Save from sin! Rise from death to life. Receive a share in Christ's identity. Live as God planned we should live. That such extravagant riches from God should be ours – entirely undeserved – is utterly beyond belief. It's his grace and love that bring it all about. Our ability even to accept God's gift and exercise faith is a gift from him. Our capacity to live and speak and work for him are fuelled and energised by his Spirit's power. This means that me-ism – our pride – is out in the cold.

With all this treasure on board there comes with it the responsibility to share it around. Recently I was with some specialists in evangelism. Each concluded we must make greater use of the Web, capitalise on modern technology. True, but do people see enough of Christ in us to want a share in God's grace?

God's New Society

*'Now in Christ Jesus you who were once far away
have been brought near' (v. 13).*

In life we sometimes feel that the 'best' usually goes to another. Somehow we don't count for much. Someone else gets all the breaks and we've got to make do. This is how it was for many in Paul's day. Religion, culture and race were barriers between people. Is it any different today?

Consider religion. When I used to take *The War Cry* (a Salvation Army paper) into the public houses often I was accosted with, 'Religion has caused more wars than anything else in the world.' Then, as now, I agree. Adherents of all three one-God faiths – Jews, Christians and Muslims – have spilt innocent blood. Why? They saw the other as the 'outsider', a threat, a rival – even an enemy. The past troubles in Northern Ireland between Protestants and Catholics and the slaughter in Iraq involving Sunni and Shia are frightening examples.

Paul's 'one *in* Christ' message now deals with a contentious issue in the Church of his day: Jews and Gentiles. At the heart of the dispute was the question of who belongs to God. The Jews regarded themselves as the 'chosen' people to the exclusion of everyone else. It came as a great shock to discover that Gentiles also are included in God's cosmic plan of reconciliation and special relationship with himself. Those who had been 'outsiders', aliens without covenant promise or hope, are now, through the blood and death of Christ, included in the circle of God's love. Jesus took the hostility and hatred into himself. When he died, it died.

Because of Christ, the walls that divided are smashed to pieces. A building where Christ is the foundation stone stands in its place. We have 'the portrait of an alienated humanity', then, 'the portrait of a peace-making Christ' and lastly 'the portrait of God's new society'.[5]

In God's new society Christ is everything and everyone counts for something. No one is out in the cold who is *in* Christ. No longer is there one favoured people. All are welcome! Together they form one body of Christ where God's Spirit lives.

God's Open Secret

*'The Message is accessible and welcoming to everyone,
across the board' (v. 6, MSG).*

In two senses Paul is a prisoner: in a Roman jail awaiting trial before
Nero because of his Christ-centred ministry to the Gentiles (Acts
28:16, 30) and as one who deeply *adored* Christ and found his real life
in Christ. True freedom was total abandonment to Christ. Paul isn't
complaining but celebrating. He genuinely counts it an honour to
suffer for Christ (Philippians 1:3–30).

Paul the prisoner remained Paul the preacher. His loss of physical
freedom fuelled his passion to proclaim the freedom found only in
Christ. We often pray for release from suffering, who can blame us?
Yet, if Paul's life is anything to go by, God does his greatest work
through our pain and we are drawn more and more into Christ. Jesus
promised three things to his disciples – that 'they would be absurdly
happy, completely fearless, and in constant trouble'.[6]

'God gave me grace . . . he allowed me to understand his secret by
giving me a direct revelation,' says Paul (see v. 3). The best discoveries
in life are a gift from God. Topping all of them is the reality that God
loves everyone *equally* in Christ. This is God's open secret. Paul never
got over the fact that God chose *him*, 'less than the least' (v. 8), to be a
channel of his grace (Galatians 2:7, 9; Romans 15:15).

Great conductor Toscanini, briefing an orchestra on a Beethoven
symphony, said: 'Gentlemen, I am nothing; you are nothing;
Beethoven is everything.' Sadly today some evangelists are more self-
promoting than Christ-adoring. Christ shone through Paul the way he
did because Paul regarded himself as nothing, while Christ was
everything. We too have been entrusted with 'the unsearchable riches
of Christ' (v. 8) to be shared in service to others.

In the 1960s the Joystrings (a beat group formed within The
Salvation Army) famously sang their songs in churches, theatres, TV
and in the red light district of Soho, London. An unforgettable song was
'It's An Open Secret' which said we can '*know* God's loving-kindness'.
God's message is 'accessible and welcoming to everyone, across the
board'.

Our world is dying to hear God's open secret. Only those who place
Christ first can tell it as it is, whatever the cost.

More or Less

∙∙

*'Set your hearts on things above . . . set your minds on things above,
not on earthly things' (vv. 1, 2).*

The apostle Paul echoes countless Scripture texts when he tells us to
set our minds on heavenly, not earthly things. That is not to say
we must be 'so heavenly minded that we are of no earthly use'. To live
safely and usefully on earth we need to be what contemporary
language calls 'streetwise', but our mindset – our philosophy, our
attitude – should be such that our gaze is fixed not on the gutter but on
the stars.

Mixture

Why is man such a mixture,
Good and bad?
It's rather
Disappointing,
Even sad!
It's always seemed to me
A trifle odd
That part of me is me
And part is God!
But each day that I live
My whole life through,
Let there be less of me
And more of you!

God's Treasure Beyond Measure

....

'I pray that out of his glorious riches he may strengthen you with power through his Spirit in your inner being' (v. 16).

My wife and I visited Phoenix, Arizona, in the USA. One day we watched as an eagle soared and glided with great ease high up in the prairie sky. In this prayer Paul, as it were, is flying in 'heavenly places'. Like an eagle carried on the thermal, he is able to view the vast, extravagant dimensions of the riches of Christ! Chest bursting with joy, he strives to articulate the indescribable.

Paul can hardly believe it! Those far from God, dubbed the 'outsiders', are now made alive *in* Christ. Each has priceless access into the very presence of Almighty God. Only one way to respond to such truth: fall on your knees before the Father of all. As a Jew he was required to stand and pray; how could he? The reality is mindboggling. Instead, he prostrates himself before God's glorious majesty! When we pray, the posture is less important than the passion, pleading and worship we bring to it.

Paul longs for the Ephesians to be 'rooted and established in love'. It is a prayer that, through the Spirit's power, they may know the boundless depths and dimensions of Christ's love (vv. 16, 19). Only the Spirit can make it happen. Only the Spirit empowers and enables the believer to know the 'deep things of God' (1 Corinthians 2:10–12). Only the Spirit brings us into line with God's will. God's love is the source by which believers are nourished. To know Christ's love is to be transformed by that love and share in the very fullness of God!

As children of our loving heavenly Father, we are urged by Paul: 'Reach out and experience the breadth! Test its length! Plumb the depths! Rise to the heights! Live full lives, full in the fullness of God' (vv. 18, 19, *MSG*). When this happens, the drive to *reach* others is powerful. To bless those who hate us, bring hope to the hopeless, offer food to the hungry and life to the dying.

On us, the Spirit has lavished God's treasure beyond measure!

Forward as One

....

'I want you to get out there and walk – better yet, run! –
on the road God called you to travel' (v. 1, MSG).

Having dealt with the heart of the Christian faith, Paul now looks for evidence of its practical application in daily life. 'No passage is more descriptive of the church in action,' says the *NIV Commentary*. The picture is of the body of Christ, made of many parts. The appeal is for movement and maturity. It's time for infants in the faith to grow up. My five-year-old granddaughter has it right when she sings, 'Move it! Move it! Move it!' No diversions, no short cuts, one way forward: Christ's way.

We are all called to mirror Christ's humility, discipline and, above all, love. It's not a case of putting up with each other but of looking out for others. We should take second place (Philippians 2:5–8). We're to be radiant with gentle sensitivity, to practise patience and, in the words of John Chrysostom, 'have a wide and big soul'.[7]

The heart of it all is this: being with Christ means loving like Christ. Most of us struggle with this requirement. Why? The concept in the song 'I did it my way' is why. But if, like Paul, we forget about ourselves and become Christ's *prisoner*, we will move forward and take others with us.

In moving forward we do so as one: 'One Master, one faith, one baptism, one God and Father of all, who rules over all, works through all, and is present in all. Everything you are and think and do is permeated with Oneness' (Ephesians 4:5, 6, *MSG*). The divided Church is largely caused by those who think they have a monopoly on truth. Individualism in faith is flawed and dangerous. We all need each other. As F. F. Bruce says: 'The higher reaches of the Christian life cannot be attained in isolation from one's fellow believers.'[8]

The grace of Christ gifts God's people with power by the Spirit. They have different roles: prophets, evangelists, pastors and teachers in parallel ministry. All matter. All have a part to play for all *belong* to the one body of Christ. By the reality of God's truth and love, we go forward as one.

Throw Away the Old –
Put On the New

···

'Fling off the dirty clothes of the old way of living, which were rotted through and through . . . put on the clean fresh clothes of the new life which was made by God's design' (vv. 22–24, JBP).

I love it when I put on a clean freshly ironed shirt – the fragrance, the feel. By contrast, one cold winter's day my wife helped peel off the foul-smelling rags of a street gentleman, while her friend bathed his swollen wounded feet. A hot meal, new clothes, and his eyes shone with hope.

Paul is dealing here with two kinds of life. One is futile, without meaning, promise or even reality. Pride and self-centredness have pushed God out of the picture. Result: the light has been turned off. 'They can't think straight anymore. Feeling no pain, they let themselves go in sexual obsession, addicted to every sort of perversion' (v. 19, *MSG*).

The other life – one in union with Christ – is transformed. Those living it walk in the light of God, their minds renewed. They have stripped off 'the old way of living' and 'put on the clean fresh clothes of the new life' from God.

We live in a society that promotes fame and fortune, and values popularity and pleasure more than sacrifice and service. The media industry both informs and shapes us with news, films and TV shows. Singers, actors and talk-show hosts along with sports celebrities occupy centre stage.

Tragically, sexual promiscuity and violence to women and children are too common. Untamed desire craves more and more satisfaction, and self-centredness rules too many people. Although sexuality and pleasure are not bad in themselves – they are, after all, gifts from God to be used in ways that honour him – they can become masters exerting a tyrannical power.

What's the answer? It is to sign up for learning at the feet of Christ and be made a new person by his power. God calls us to throw away the old and put on the new; to exchange rags for royal robes. This way the old me gives way to a new me (vv. 22–24; Colossians 3:9–11; Romans 6:3, 6). And what is the new me? The very character of God *in* me!

New Life of Love

....

*'Live a life of love, just as Christ loved us and gave
himself up for us' (5:2).*

Tell the truth. Keep your head. Give up stealing and get a job. Mind your language. It sounds like a list of instructions. It is. We're talking ethics here. The Christian life based on Christ's love is always accountable for its behaviour. Its top priority, according to the *NIV Commentary*, is to 'reject what destroys community and promote what builds community'. This community 'is intimately related to each other in Christ', although at times you'd hardly think so, the way some people go on. Despite God's truth and love, Paul declares their track record a failure. Let's be honest, at times we're all poor examples at home and unattractive adverts for Christianity in society.

Instead of reflecting the new being in Christ, we sometimes lack transparency, telling people what they want to hear if it works to our advantage, and shrinking from the truth when it's costly. Sometimes we exaggerate to enhance ourselves at someone else's expense, distorting reality. And, as John Mackay says, lying to ourselves or to others 'delivers a stab into the very vitals of the Body of Christ . . . there is no place in the Christian ethic for the well intentioned lie.'[9] Only truth builds people and society. It comes from God. Without it, nothing's sure, nothing survives (see John 8:31, 32).

Addressing Christians, Paul says there's to be no more bitterness, rage, anger, brawling, slander or malice. Anger here is not referring to anger in response to such things as poverty, injustice, lies, racism and abuse. Rather it's the destructive sort that lashes out with harsh uncontrolled temper. When two people fail to reconcile their differences it grieves God the Holy Spirit, invites hostility and destroys human relations. Such antagonism is a vice, and an enemy to God's people.

How do we deal with an enemy, either from within or without? With kindness, understanding, forgiveness and, above all, love – the 'same sort of love which Christ gives us and which he perfectly expressed when he gave himself up for us in sacrifice to God' (4:32, *JBP*). In this life of love we are to 'watch what God does, and then you do it' (v. 1, *MSG*).

You are Light in the Lord

'The bright light of Christ makes your way plain. So no more stumbling around. Get on with it!' (v. 9, MSG).

The starting line is the light and love of Christ. It will take believers to the finishing point. The in-between bit can be messy. Christians, says Paul, are surrounded with alien lifestyles: sexual promiscuity, sickening greed, dirty talk. These must not form any part of their lives. Once 'darkness' now 'light', they are to do what pleases Christ.

This passage could have been written to members of any church. Why, even in Christian fellowships, is there sometimes sexual sin, bad language and greed? Sexual sin trades on pride, power and pleasure. Foul talk lowers the moral temperature. Before you know it, obscenities and coarse joking are acceptable. Untamed desire leads to greed for possessions and power. Such greed cramps and masters our every move. The advertising and gambling industries profit from the 'must have, must own' of our lives. Twisted sex, dirty words and selfish living are all variations of idolatry. God will judge severely, warns Paul.

Into all of this comes Christ's transforming light, shining through his people (v. 8). From him we receive a new being. We are stamped with his identity. Love, goodness and truth define us as 'we shine like stars in the universe' (Philippians 2:15), confronting the darkness of our street and society.

We must steer clear of the dark side, and reach out to people, practising distinctiveness, not separation. As the saying has it, we must hate the sin, but love the sinner. Today the word 'sin' has all but disappeared from common usage but remains a personal and social deadly reality. Only God, by his light and truth, is able to destroy the power of sin and save the world and its people (Romans 6:19–23; John 3:16, 19–21).

We have here a wake-up call. The race is on, there's no time to lose. The light is shining. The darkness can't escape it. God's children of light see things as they really are. We live with the danger of the world's values rubbing off on us but we know how to overcome: by putting Christ first! That way *we* are light in the Lord.

Mind How You Go!

*'Make the best use of your time . . . firmly grasp what you know to be
the will of God' (vv. 16, 17, JBP).*

We live in desperate times. What's new? Does human nature ever
change? Not unless God does the job. The apostle Paul is pressing
here for believers to make the best use of time. The clock is ticking.
The days are evil. Lives are wasted on drunkenness 'which leads to
debauchery'. This is mindless and irresponsible waste (Romans 13:12,
13). Worse still, such a life bypasses being 'filled with the Spirit' of God.

Alternatively, where the Spirit flows through us everything else falls
into place. Inspiration to 'sing and make music' pleasing to God springs
from our amazing walk with him. Christ is the centre and circum-
ference of everything. Knowing and doing God's will, not our own, is
the greatest thing in the world. The outcome is exuberant praise and
'thanks to God' twinned with mutual respect and submission to each
other (Colossians 3:15-17; 4:2; 1 Peter 1:3-5; 4:8-10; Philippians 2:3;
Matthew 23:12).

Our society is in a big hurry. Gadgetry does much for us but we're
busier than ever. Our lives are packed with activity but how much time
do we give to God? Some indulge themselves in alcohol. While con-
sumption of alcoholic beverage is not a sin, drunkenness is. Whether
binge drinking or drunken drivers, the end result can be devastating.
The point made by Paul is that debauchery results from excessive and
wasteful indulgence.

The truth is, we are made for God's Spirit to inhabit. All we are, all
we hope to be, is brought into focus by the Spirit, who is no optional
extra or secondary being in the Godhead. He's no less than the Bringer
of Life! When he comes to us he is not alone. God the Father and Son
are with him, in us. When this happens, we are in the centre of God's
will. For this reason we act with wisdom, make the best use of our
time, revere one another and celebrate in a chorus of praise and
thanksgiving to our great God.

To ponder:
The greatest thing in life is to *know* and to *do* the will of God.

In Charge

....

*'Put to death . . . whatever belongs to your earthly nature . . .
you used to walk in these ways, in the life you once lived. But now
you must rid yourselves of all such things' (vv. 5, 7, 8).*

God's gift to humankind of free will rules out an easy life when it comes to making big decisions. Unredeemed human nature sometimes seems to offer only 'fight or flight' alternatives in difficult circumstances, and few moral dilemmas are solved by either course. Running away can be no more honourable than using force – physical or emotional – to emerge the 'winner'. Christ triumphed over evil by his willingness to accept the cross. Sometimes we have to do the same.

Ego

The 'me' in me
Insists upon attention
In ways, if you don't mind,
I will not mention.
It even tries to
Take away your throne,
And rule over my mini-world
Alone!
I've tried to starve this ego
But it feeds
Upon itself!
No nourishment it needs.

Give me the grit
To down it and defy it;
To take the nails and daily
Crucify it!

Love like Christ

....

*'Husbands, love your wives, just as Christ loved the
church and gave himself up for her . . . and the wife must
respect her husband' (vv. 25, 33).*

What makes a successful marriage? When a church goes wrong,
how can it be put right? Two questions, one answer. For the
couple, for the community of faith, the answer lies in loving the way
Christ loves. A fragmented church, like a fractured relationship, is due
to the absence of Christ. Paul's primary subject here is not really
marriage; he uses that as an analogy for 'the marriage of Christ and his
Church' (v. 32, JBP). The love of Christ, his saving work and his
constant care for the Church are pre-eminent.

Does this mean the weddings we've attended when this passage was
read: 'Wives, submit to your husbands . . . Husbands, love your wives'
(vv. 22, 25) had it wrong? No. Although these verses might appear to
order that husbands should rule and wives submit, this is a gross
misinterpretation. Husbands have no privileged position. Wives are
not inferior. At work here is mutual submission and support. 'The
husband provides leadership to his wife the way Christ does to his
church, not by domineering but by cherishing' (v. 24, MSG). Loving her
as much as he loves himself and as much as Christ loves the Church is
a huge responsibility.

And wives are to understand and support their husbands in ways
similar to the way the Church submits to Christ. It has nothing to do
with one marriage partner being better than the other. It has everything to do with equal yet distinct roles in Christ. In marriage or being
single, all Christians are to act towards each other as Christ acts
(Romans 12:10).

In our relationship with Christ, the Church and each other, there's
only one Head and that's Christ. But while Head, he's also the servant
of all, and so must we be to each other (Matthew 20:26–28). If we are
to love like Christ then we should take note: 'Christ's love makes the
church whole. His words evoke her beauty. Everything he does and
says is designed to bring the best out of her, dressing her in dazzling
white silk, radiant with holiness' (Ephesians 5:26–28, MSG).

A Family in the Lord

'Children, obey your parents in the Lord . . . "Honour your father and mother . . . that it may go well with you" . . . Fathers, do not exasperate your children . . . bring them up in the training and instruction of the Lord' (vv. 1–4).

'Apart from religious influence,' writes Dr Billy Graham, 'the family is the most important unit in society . . . [it] can never exert its proper influence while ignoring the biblical standard.'[10] The standard is Christ. We are not talking merely about ethics but about family life being 'in Christ', with parents exerting patient and loving discipline 'in the Lord'. In that way, children can model their lives on their parents' good and godly influence.

Where fathers 'exasperate' their children, they're clearly failing to live up to the high ideal outlined in these verses. As for the children, they are not free to have it all their own way. Like it or not, they are commanded to obey their parents – something entirely justified where parents are modelling Christ to their children.

D. L. Moody said, 'A man ought to live so that everybody knows he is a Christian and most of all, his *family* ought to know.'[11] Sadly, at times we operate a double persona: one private, one public. The 'nice' person people see in public can be quite different at home, where our loved ones see us as we really are. All of us – adults and children – must own up to our failures and allow the Lord to guide us.

Some Christian parents can rejoice that their adult children follow the Lord's leading. Others, despite their poured-out love and prayers over the years, suffer the ongoing heartbreak of a child who has turned their back on Christ, sometimes to the extent of rejecting all their parents stand for. Why? Only God knows.

Homes in which family members use and abuse each other for their own ends release into the wider community an explosive cocktail of anger, violence and abuse. 'Sins of the fathers' *are* sometimes passed on from generation to generation. When parents fail, often the children do so as well. John Locke said, 'Parents wonder why the streams are bitter when they themselves have poisoned the fountain.'[12]

The best family is one 'in the Lord', characterised by mutual respect, integrity of faith and, above all, love.

I Honour You as I Honour Christ

··

*'Serve wholeheartedly, as if you were serving the Lord,
not men . . . slave or free' (vv. 7, 8).*

It is estimated that in Paul's day more than a third of the population were slaves. The culture and economy rode on the backs of those with few or no rights. Many were treated harshly, some condemned to death with no appeal. By contrast others held key posts in institutions and households. In both poor and rich families some slaves were regarded as valued members of the family.

Who owned who? Legally, the slave was in the service of his or her master. But in Christian households both slave and free were bound to Christ himself. Each was required to submit to the other. In that respect they were no different from everyone else in the Christian community (6:7–8).

By this, the slavery system was stood on its head. Each was to obey 'the *real* master, Christ' (v. 5, *MSG*). Submission on the part of a slave owner was revolutionary. Paul insisted that all believers, like himself, should be slaves not of people but Christ – the one who 'made himself nothing' (1 Corinthians 7:21–23; Romans 1:1, 2; Philippians 2:7). Had this ideal happened, the Greco-Roman world might have been so different and the shameful transatlantic trade in human cargo might never have taken place.

Dr Martin Luther King's 'I have a dream' speech on 28 August 1963 urged 'let freedom ring' for all. The fight for freedom goes on. People still are dehumanised. Insidious forces are at work. The white slave trade and illicitly obtained human body parts today plunge thousands of people into misery and despair. Far from honouring human dignity, acknowledging that each person possesses God's image, trafficked people are perceived as objects of sexual pleasure and cheap labour.

The Christian's work ethic and human relations happen in the presence of Christ. Whatever we do to others, we do to Christ (Matthew 25:40). The believer is not favoured above the non-believer. Each has equal standing before God (James 2:1–13). All should have the best we can give. Unless we respect and value all, we *cannot* honour Christ. Now there's a challenge and no mistake!

The Fight Goes On

··

*'God is strong, and he wants you strong . . . to stand up to
everything . . . This is for keeps, a life-or-death fight to the finish
against the Devil and all his angels' (vv. 10, 11, 13, MSG).*

Put on God's armour and his characteristics, and you become a new
you, 'like God in true righteousness and holiness' (4:24). God's
designer attire fits us perfectly. His power and strength can be ours,
not just to help us 'feel good' but to do battle against what William
Shakespeare has called 'the slings and arrows of outrageous fortune'.
We must take evil seriously, not playing around with magic, musing on
Satan or dabbling in astrology.

We refuse to rest while the world bleeds. The open wounds of
oppression and exploitation, the brutalising and bestial treatment
of human beings, the shame of the starving and the horror of the lost
must grab our attention. We cannot be a Christian without being a
soldier.

Who's the enemy? Not people, not authorities but schemes, philos-
ophies, systems and ideologies designed to work against humanity,
devaluing and destroying it. The fight that goes on is the fight against
evil and the evil one. From mass murder of other ethnic groups to
personal failure, declaring 'I wasn't myself when I did that' reveals the
undeniable reality of evil.

In modern culture the reality of the devil is less acceptable than once
it was. This is not a good thing. As someone has said, 'Satan's greatest
weapon is to convince the world he does not exist.' This much is
certain: the power of darkness is a time bomb which can bring
destruction on nations and individuals, though in the end, it will be
defeated (Matthew 25:41; Revelation 17:8; 20:10).

What of now? This is God's world. Only he is in charge. Forces
ranged against him are being, and will be, defeated (Luke 10:18;
Revelation 12:7-17). Never forget Satan, unlike God, can't be
everywhere at once. His powers are limited. His days are numbered.
Look to God. Don't focus on the evil one. When we turn our eyes from
God, blindness takes us over.

Paul urges us to be 'strong in the Lord and his mighty power'. The
sounds of Christ's victory vibrate in our hearts. Yes, the fight goes on
but the victory has already been won!

God's Armour of Protection, Power and Prayer

··

'Stand firm . . . take . . . the sword of the Spirit, which is the word of God. And pray in the Spirit' (vv. 14, 17, 18).

Action stations! Not only is there no discharge in this war, there is no going it alone. The enemy is fierce and cunning and the challenges on every side call for constant vigilance. No one can win, or even survive, without the correct equipment. No victory will be secured without the Spirit's power. Prayer and the gospel are the most formidable weapons of God's soldier.

Like soldiers, we are to mount a serious campaign, take the high ground and hold it at all costs. This is not for the faint-hearted. Paul uses the analogy of the Roman soldier with his armour and sword. The soldier's belt, breastplate, footwear, shield, helmet and sword signify truth, righteousness, peace, faith, salvation and God's Word.

Protection from enemy attack and power to defeat the enemy rest on two factors: God's protective armoury (Isaiah 11:5; 59:17; 52:7) and the 'sword of the Spirit, which is the word of God'.

Standing firm, engaging the enemy and winning the battle calls for commitment to prayer. Paul's entreaty to 'pray in the Spirit' is not about speaking in tongues. Rather, he connects it with being filled with the Spirit's strength and persevering when the going gets tough (Ephesians 6:13, 16; 5:18; Philippians 4:6–7). Prayer also produces the power to be fearless when proclaiming the mystery of the gospel (Ephesians 6:19, 20), which is made known by God through revelation.

May God help us to take our stand for Christ, boldly and in the power of his mighty Spirit! May he teach us not just to pray our 'wish list' but to identify with his own will and purpose in every circumstance of life.

Someone has said, 'Prayer is a kind of spiritual breathing.' We need to pray not just in our quiet 'set-aside' times but also through the toil and grind of dark, doubt-filled days, and in the thick of battle when peace is a distant dream. May we 'not be anxious', for the Spirit is with us and his peace guards our hearts (Philippians 4:6–7; Romans 8:26).

The Message and the Messenger

'Tychicus . . . my good friend . . . is certainly a dependable servant of the Master! I've sent him . . . to cheer you on in your faith. Good-bye, friends. Love mixed with faith be yours from God the Father and from the Master, Jesus Christ. Pure grace and nothing but grace be with all who love our Master, Jesus Christ' (vv. 21–24, MSG).

When you send a letter or package and want to be sure it arrives intact, you pay an extra cost for 'special delivery'. The apostle Paul knew that Tychicus was someone of exceptional character and Christian standing, and therefore chose him as his messenger to Ephesus. The letter would be delivered by hand, along with a verbal report on the imprisoned Paul in Rome (vv. 21, 22).

Typically, Paul ignores his own pain as a prisoner to cheer and encourage the believers. He knew about suffering but also knew God would always be there. He further knew how to forget about himself and focus on the pain of others with Christ-like compassion (4:1; 2 Corinthians 1:4).

When, as a young man, I was commissioned as a Salvation Army officer in London's Royal Albert Hall, I heard the then leader of The Salvation Army, General Frederick Coutts, utter words which are forever indelibly printed on my mind and subsequently enriched my ministry: 'The message is greater than the messenger!' That's it. When the messenger delivers the message taking Christ as his model, then peace, love and grace reach their target.

The end of this letter links with the beginning (1:3). The benediction emphasises 'God the Father and the Lord Jesus Christ' (vv. 23, 24) as the source of peace, love, faith and grace. The believers have one glorious God and Father and are blessed beyond measure. God has given us all we need. We are all called and commissioned to live out in action to others what we have become in Christ.

May 'pure grace and nothing but grace be with all who love our Master, Jesus Christ' (v. 21, MSG).

To pray:
Lord, thank you for giving us yourself without reserve! Teach us to follow your example. Grant us your grace that we may give ourselves away to others and, in service, see Christ in all. Amen.

Spiritual Garments

'As God's chosen people . . . clothe yourselves with compassion, kindness, humility, gentleness and patience . . . Forgive as the Lord forgave you. And over all these virtues put on love' (vv. 12, 14).

What God requires of us is not that we deny our humanity, our individuality, our weakness, but that we transform these things by the Christian qualities that will clothe our 'nakedness' with such spiritual garments as compassion and patience. The beauty we then display to those who meet us will not be our own, but our Lord's.

Beauty

I cannot see your beauty
But I sense it.
My mind is touched by yours
If not embraced.
You glide alongside
When I least expect it
And all my spent-out forces
Are replaced.
But with the strength you give me,
And the patience,
Grant something of
Your unseen grace to me.
Then men will sense
Your beauty in my nature,
Your loveliness
In my humanity!

The Christian and
Undeserved Suffering

Readings from 1 Peter

Introduction

Few experiences in life more openly reveal our characters than our reaction to innocent suffering. It is hard enough to bear the painful consequences of wrongdoing, but to face undeserved suffering uncomplainingly, even graciously, is infinitely harder. This is the major theme of Peter's letter.

Peter was writing to Christians who, if not actually experiencing persecution for their faith, were expecting to. Their main feared antagonist was Nero, the Roman emperor, whose unpredictable ravings were frequently against the innocent. Writing probably from Rome, symbolically described as 'Babylon', in AD 64, the apostle outlines how the Christian should face adversity. His letter has remained one of the best loved in the entire New Testament, and is full of insight for us.

These daily readings are from the pen of the then Major Fred Brown and were first published in *The Soldier's Armoury* (forerunner of *Words of Life*) in January 1962.

For the Sunday readings, John Gowans continues to provide a prayer-poem with a selected Bible passage.

Chosen to Obey

*'Chosen according to the foreknowledge of God the Father,
through the sanctifying work of the Spirit, for obedience to
Jesus Christ and sprinkling by his blood' (v. 2).*

To be chosen by God is both an honour and a responsibility, which explains why those who are most used in his service are also the most humble. Robert Raikes, prominent Sunday-school pioneer, once led a young friend to the spot in a back street in Gloucester, England, where he had been inspired to start his first school.

Deeply moved, and reverently uncovering his head, he said, 'Pause here. This is the spot on which I stood when I saw the destitution of the children and the desecration of the Sabbath. As I asked, "Can nothing be done?" a voice answered, "Try." I did try, and see what God has wrought. I can never pass by the spot where the word *try* came so powerfully into my mind without lifting up my hands and heart to heaven in gratitude to God.'

We, too, have been chosen 'according to the foreknowledge of God' and for a basic twofold purpose: to be sanctified or consecrated by the Holy Spirit; and for obedience to Christ.

This latter truth is illustrated by reference to the 'sprinkling of blood' ceremony associated with the covenant relationship between Israel and God (see Exodus 24:1-8). The covenant was valid only as Israel obeyed.

Christ's blood was shed for us, but the intimate relationship with God this makes possible is contingent upon *our* obedience.

To ponder:
'The commands of Jesus are never polite recommendations; they demand obedience, albeit it is recognised that true obedience is precisely that which man in his own strength is unable to render.'

Bishop Stephen Neill

Facing Adversity

*'You are guarded by the power of God operating
through your faith' (v. 5, JBP).*

'The things that try us most', wrote Robert Rainy to Alexander Whyte, 'are the experiences which are the most indispensable of all for us.' Such wisdom is hard to believe, and harder to act upon, particularly when trials actually come.

Persecution, called by Peter 'the trial of your faith', was expected by the Christians to whom this letter was addressed. How were they to meet it? The apostle, by now a veteran of the spiritual battlefield, gave them rich encouragement:

If adversity would prove their faith (v. 7), *it would also prove God's keeping power* (v. 5). When Polycarp, saintly Bishop of Smyrna, was about to be martyred, he stopped his persecutors nailing him to the stake at which he was to be burned alive. 'It is unnecessary,' he said. 'He who gives me strength to endure in the flame will enable me to stand firm.'

God's power and our faith can still do the seemingly impossible. Imprisoned by the Nazis, a German pastor declared: 'I will somehow hold out physically, no matter how long it may last.' But he knew that more than human resolve was required. 'During these years', he continued, 'in sheer terror we may sometimes have felt as though we were falling into the bottomless abyss. But there is a power that sustains us; we are borne up by God the Father's everlasting arms.'

For every experience in life, we should heed John Wesley's dictum: 'The power of God is there. Use it.'

Though I have never heard thee tread
The crowded streets where now I live,
Nor 'mid the people watched thee give
Thy benison, as broken bread;
I know and love thee as thou art
Within the chancel of my heart!
Albert Orsborn

Revelation

••

'The prophets of old did their utmost to discover and obtain this
salvation' (v. 10, JBP).

'An atheist I never was', wrote Charles Kingsley to someone in
mental perplexity, 'but in my early life I wandered through many
doubts and vain attempts to explain to myself the riddle of life and this
world, till I found no explanation was so complete as the one which
one had learned at one's mother's knee.' Kingsley found the truth,
despite his doubts, because he never stopped seeking for it.

God reveals himself only to the diligent seeker (v. 10). Far too often, we
complain that spiritual revelation never comes, without recognising
the reason why – our moral and mental laziness. Observed Albert
Einstein: 'There is such a thing as a passionate desire to understand,
just as there is a passionate love for music. This passion is common
with children, but it usually vanishes as they grow up.'

Explaining Einstein's greatness, Antonina Vallentin, his biographer,
commented: 'This passion never left him.' But has this passion to
understand, to know more and more of God, left us?

God reveals himself always through the Spirit of Christ (v. 11). He
indwelt the Old Testament prophets and inspired them to speak even
more than they themselves could realise of his sufferings and glory;
and still he alone makes God real to us, for where there is beauty and
truth and aspiration, there is the Spirit of Christ.

Could this fact – that revelation comes most readily to the diligent
seeker whose mind is saturated with the Gospels – explain our lack of
insight and conviction?

Holy Living

....

*'Be holy in every detail of your lives, as he, whose servants
you are, is holy' (v. 15, BBE).*

Peter has some down-to-earth advice, all in verse 13, about how to
live victoriously.

We need to 'gird up the loins' of our mind. Unless oriental robes were
neatly folded and tucked into a girdle, they wrapped themselves about
the wearer's legs, seriously impeding his progress. This was the picture
Peter had in mind when he told his readers to 'gird up the loins' of their
mind. He would probably have urged us to 'roll up the sleeves' of our
mind.

Slovenly thinking and noble living never go together. Our thought
life, our imagination, our secret affections, of which other people
possibly know nothing, could explain our spiritual malnutrition.
Holiness means health, wholeness.

We need to 'be sober'. A person can be intoxicated by more than
alcohol, which is one reason why we say that some people are sober-
minded, meaning they have stability and balanced judgment. 'Be on
your guard', exhorted J. H. Jowett, 'against everything which is
creative of heaviness, and which may put your senses into a perilous
sleep.' Stupor of soul is a dangerous condition.

We need to 'hope to the end'. Now this is not the same as being hopeful
or hoping for the best. It means seeing present trials in the light of
future glory; of making every decision against the background of God's
ultimate judgment. Some people see no further than the end of their
nose, and their vision rarely extends beyond the immediate. One
frequent result is their early gain at the cost of ultimate disaster.

We must seek to live in the light of our eternal hope.

Costly Caring

'Now that you have, by obeying the truth, made your souls clean enough for a genuine love of your fellows, see that you do love each other, fervently and from the heart' (v. 22, JBP).

When a person really believes the gospel – look at its fundamental teaching in vv. 17–21 – their life issues in spontaneous caring for their fellows: 'unfeigned love of the brethren' is the natural expression of personal salvation. Bertrand Russell, the philosopher, described a fellow undergraduate as a man with a passionate love for mankind and an intense dislike for most individual men.

How like some of us! Salvationists sing so feelingly the chorus:

> Love I ask for, love I claim,
> A dying love like thine,
> A love that feels for all the world;
> Saviour, give me a love like thine.

For all the world! Yet sometimes we do not love even our neighbours, workmates and friends deeply enough and for long enough.

Costly and steady caring depends upon what we believe about God. He was Redeemer before he was Creator, for the sacrifice of Christ was 'foreordained before the foundation of the world' (v. 20, AMP); and there we have a picture of the compassionate heart of God which, coupled with the cost of our redemption, indicates the divine assessment of human personality.

We shall only share Christ's sacrificial giving for humankind when we share his understanding of the nature of God.

To ponder:
Faith in God that does not express itself in compassionate and practical concern is more belief in an impersonal Creator than in a heavenly Father.

Spiritual Growth

*'Like newly born children, thirst for the pure, spiritual milk
to make you grow up to salvation' (v. 2, JMT).*

Christian discipleship can exist only as a 'function of pilgrimage'. In other words, growth is essential. Indeed, few things are more pathetic or ominous than stunted spirituality. Knowing this, the apostle, characteristically with his feet on the ground, makes a twofold emphasis.

To 'grow up' in Christ demands fierce renunciation (v. 1). Notice which sins are specifically mentioned: 'Every trace of ill-will and deceitfulness, your affectations, the grudges you bore, and all the slanderous talk' (v. 1, *RKT*); 'All evil and deceit, all pretence and jealousy and slander' (v. 1, *JBP*).

The list is formidable, but nevertheless 'respectable'! Apparently Christians have always had more trouble with sins of the spirit than of the flesh. The apostle, like his Master, knew that envy and a gossiping tongue were more difficult to overcome and therefore more spiritually serious than drunkenness and gambling. We must take this insight to heart.

To 'grow up' in Christ demands disciplined Bible study (v. 2). Peter refers to the 'milk' and Paul to the 'meat' of the Word, each of them to underline an essential of spiritual development. If we have 'tasted that the Lord is good' (v. 3), says Peter, we shall want to renounce every hindrance and nourish our faith on the Word of God. But this works the other way too. If we practise a healthy renunciation and give adequate attention to our Bibles, our spiritual palates will become increasingly sensitive.

A Divine Nudge

••

*'Whatever you do, work at it with all your heart, as working
for the Lord, not for men . . . It is the Lord Christ you
are serving' (vv. 23, 24).*

Whole-heartedness is an attractive quality. It's something more than enthusiasm, or energy – for even bountiful quantities of those might still be less than our all. Working with all our heart, as Paul urges us here, is to follow the example of the widow who put all she had into the temple treasury. To others her contribution was a negligible amount, but because she held nothing back it was honoured by God. Sometimes we need a nudge from God to remind us that we are capable of more.

Push and Prod

I wish you'd push me
Sometimes when I'm slow
To do the things I should,
For you must know
Inertia's strongest
When I should move fast
And, all too soon,
The chance to act is past.

I want to work
But I've a lazy streak;
The spirit's willing but
The flesh is weak.
Stir me to action,
Would you be so kind?
And when I need it
Prod me from behind!

Priests unto God

....

'It is for you now to demonstrate the goodness of him who has called you out of darkness into his amazing light' (v. 9, JBP).

Of all the truths here available for the unhurried reader, we have room to focus on only one – we are a 'royal priesthood' (v. 9). The Latin word for priest is *pontifex*, which means 'bridge-builder', and this is what we are all called to be.

Robert L. Stevenson, in his search for health, built a house on a hilltop in Samoa. He made friends with the people and did his best to care for them. There was no road from the little seaport up to his house so, out of gratitude for his generous friendship, the people set to work to make one. They gave it a name which means 'The road of the loving heart'. By this road they could go to him and he come down to them.

As priests unto God, we must build a 'road', erect a 'bridge', between ourselves and the multitudes outside the influence of organised religion. Such materials as prayer, quiet industry, pen and paper, a bunch of flowers, a handshake, a smile, uncompromising loyalty to principle and, most of all, a growing love for God and people will be needed. The work will not be spectacular, but its tone and consistency will give expression to our belief in the priesthood of all believers.

Florence Allshorn tells of a Royal Air Force pilot who said to a Christian: 'Don't try to help me, or preach to me or tell me what I ought to think yet. Don't work for my salvation. Show me yours!'

....

I'm set apart for Jesus,
To be a king and priest;
His life in me increases,
Upon his love I feast.
From evil separated,
Made holy by his blood,
My all is consecrated
Unto the living God.
          William Pearson

Freedom to Choose Slavery

'Free men, but the liberty you enjoy is not to be made a pretext for wrongdoing; it is to be used in God's service' (v. 16, RKT).

For numerous reasons, early Christians were slandered and finally viciously persecuted. Peter here tells them that such antagonism is best answered by noble living. The word 'conversation' (v. 12, *KJV*) means more than verbal exchanges. It refers to a person's whole conduct, every aspect of his or her living, which, says the apostle, should be 'honest', a word translated by J. B. Phillips as 'good and right'.

A danger is that Christians, misinterpreting the meaning of their new-found freedom in Christ, should use their liberty as 'a pretext for wrongdoing', failing to see that they are free only to choose to be slaves. Paradoxically this choice alone guarantees true freedom, a truism the world is taking a long time to learn.

There stepped onto the platform of a huge auditorium in Minneapolis in 1957 the impressive figure of Bishop Ordass of Hungary, then recently released after six-and-a-half years' detention for his faith. In halting tones he told his story – always in the third person, such was his humility – describing himself as 'an ageing disciple of Jesus Christ'. Then came an unforgettable sentence: 'He would like to say that when he was in bondage, in the most literal sense of the word, Christ gave him royal freedom.'

To ponder:
'I used to think that "liberty" was freedom to get what I wanted. I know now that liberty is freedom to give what God wants, what my neighbour needs.'

Father Andrew

Getting on with People

•••

'If when you do right and suffer for it you bear it patiently, this is an acceptable thing to God' (v. 20, FWT).

One of the main reasons for unhappiness in almost every realm of life is strained human relationships. People cannot get on together. Misunderstandings cause friction; the innocent suffer; the insensitive are unconsciously hurtful; the conscientious are exploited.

Sometimes, alas, unreconciled Christians deny their spiritual heritage and disgrace the cause of Christ. In today's verses, Peter gives some challenging counsel for such situations.

Converted slaves were apparently taking advantage of their Christian masters and – more serious because there was no possible redress – many such converts were being ill-treated (v. 18). When similar situations develop today, what should be the Christian's attitude? The apostle, pointing to our supreme example, leaves no doubt about the answer: we should maintain a spirit of unyielding goodwill, completely devoid of self-pity. Even if a protest must be made, its motive should be free of personal animosity.

Humanly speaking, this is, of course, beyond us, which is why Peter relates such a demand to the centralities of our faith. Woe betide the individual who tries to produce moral 'fruits' without spiritual 'roots'!

Patiently to bear innocent suffering, to face abuse, to be misunderstood, is beyond unaided human resources. We need more than even the example of Christ to help us. We need Christ himself. And he is always with those who, though personally provoked, remain peacemakers.

Winning Unconverted Loved Ones

'You are not to adorn yourselves on the outside . . . but inside, in the heart, with the immortal beauty of a gentle, modest spirit, which in the sight of God is of rare value' (vv. 3, 4, JMT).

These verses, concerned with the relationship between husband and wife, have a much wider application; for here is guidance about the attitude of the Christian toward the unconverted, particularly unconverted relatives.

In the ancient world, a man owned his wife in much the same way as he possessed his cattle and plough. If he changed his religion, then automatically his family changed theirs. But for a wife independently to change her religion was unheard of, hence the plight of the converted housewife whose husband did not share her faith.

Peter advises that such a woman's first responsibility is to be a good wife. She should be characterised by submissiveness ('voluntary selflessness'), purity and 'reverent behaviour', resulting in what Dr William Barclay finely calls the 'silent preaching of a lovely life'.

Likewise, the husband has obligations. He should be understanding, gentle and look upon his partner as a spiritual fellow-heir. Anything less will mean that his prayers are hindered (v. 7), for nothing stands between a man and his prayers more than broken or strained relationships. It is impossible, for instance, for a man to be a good Christian and a bad or difficult husband.

To ponder:
'The secret of happy marriage lies first in loving one another a lot, but even more in loving many other things together.'

Frances Wilkinson[13]

Pity or Contempt?

....

*'You should all be of one mind living like brothers with
true love and sympathy for each other, generous and
courageous at all times' (v. 8, JBP).*

Apart from our individual lives, the fellowship to which we belong
should be marked by such qualities as unity ('all of one mind'),
compassion, love, pity, courtesy, forgiveness and dauntless goodwill.
Ronald Knox translates verse 9: 'I would see you tender-hearted,
modest, and humble, not repaying injury with injury, or hard words
with hard words, but blessing those who curse you.'

Consider today the essential nature of Christian pity. In *Private World
of Pain*, Grace Stuart, almost a lifelong sufferer from arthritis, makes
this revealing comment:

We receive too much of that coin of pity whose other face is
contempt. Contempt – and yet perhaps not always quite contempt.
Should one say, rather, an urgent, unconscious need to see
someone else as in any way down in order that the looker-on may
feel himself to be in some way up? Our fond belief that we do not
kick a man when he is down may have as one of its functions the
concealment of the fact that we need people who are down in
order to have someone to kick.[14]

Later she refers to those who 'need their pity of us, their morbid
interest in us, for unhappy ends of their own'. Here speaks a woman
who obviously has suffered at the hands of well-meaning but
insensitive 'sympathisers'.

Pity does issue in sympathy, but never in sentiment; it is costly,
often making severe demands. Indeed, *easy* pity is really the contempt
of which Grace Stuart rightly complains. We must make time to ponder
the masculine compassion of Christ, which always expressed itself,
through his vicarious suffering, in sensitive caring.

How to Testify

••

*'Be ready at any time to give a quiet and reverent answer
to any man who wants a reason for the hope that you
have within you' (v. 15, JBP).*

Peter's guidance about how to witness for Christ is as valid today as
ever.

The Christian should be *ready* to witness. This refers not only to
specific preparation but also to the spirit in which the believer faces
daily responsibility. A man is ready to witness not because he has the
right words formulated in his mind but because he has secretly maintained 'the spiritual glow' (Romans 12:11, *JMT*). Such an individual is
never caught on the hop.

The Christian's witness should be reasonable. He is called upon to
give a *reason* for the hope within him. This does demand intelligent
reading and hard thinking; but in these days of inexpensive paperbacks
no Christian can be excused for not being informed about their faith.

The Christian's witness should be given with *meekness*, translated as
'gently' by Moffatt and 'courteously' by Knox. We can be forthright
without raising our voices and becoming bigoted, dogmatic or intoler-
ant. Conviction loses none of its winsomeness or authority by being
'quiet' – the word used by J. B. Phillips, meaning gracious and patient.

The Christian's witness should be given with *reverence*. There is a
danger that testimony can become cheap, slick, a matter of little more
than words. A believer called upon frequently to witness at open-air
meetings, for instance, can merely talk, not testify. The element of
wonder should be safeguarded in testimony, and this will help to avoid
argument or theological wrangling.

Speak Up

··

'Therefore, brothers, we have an obligation . . . For you did not receive
a spirit that makes you a slave again to fear' (vv. 12, 15).

We don't much like being obligated to someone. It takes away our freedom to be free agents. Or so we think. The truth is, our Christian faith frees us up to be the people God wants us to be, and the people we ourselves want to be in our best moments. Sometimes the obligation on us is to speak out against the wrong we see. And sometimes there's a cost to that. But God offers us the grace we need.

Conformity

I hate to be less
Than popular,
I like to be liked.
That's bad?
And sometimes
It keeps me silent
When I should speak out.
That's sad!

Forgive me
When I've said nothing,
Just to stay one of the gang,
Betrayed what I most
Believe in,
And let the truth go hang!

I want to speak out
When I should, Lord,
So give me the nerve I need.
And if I must suffer for it
You'll grant me the grace.
Agreed?

The Sovereignty of Christ

*'It may be God's will that we suffer for doing right; better that,
than for doing wrong' (v. 17, RKT).*

In considering this doctrine of the creed – 'He descended into hell' –
we must surely recognise the folly of dogmatism. These verses in
Peter's first letter are so surrounded by mystery that only stupidity
would claim an infallible interpretation. There is, nevertheless, one
certain aspect of their meaning which we do well to ponder: Christ is
Lord, even in hell!

What else could Paul have meant when he wrote: 'At the name of
Jesus every knee should bow, of things in heaven, and things in earth,
and things under the earth' (Philippians 2:10, *KJV*)? And what about
the triumphant picture of Revelation 5:13 (*KJV*): 'Every creature which
is in Heaven and on the earth, and under the earth . . . heard I saying,
Blessing, and honour, and glory, and power, be unto him that sitteth
upon the throne, and unto the Lamb for ever and ever'?

The devil himself is under Christ's sovereignty and therefore finally
incapable of defeating his purposes. What better realisations to steady
our faith in these turbulent days?

The Lord our refuge is
And ever will remain;
Since he has made us his
He will our cause maintain.
In vain our enemies oppose,
For God is stronger than his foes.
attributed to Samuel Barnard

Motive

*'Serve one another with the particular gifts God has given
each of you, as faithful dispensers of the magnificently
varied grace of God' (v. 10, JBP).*

With insight into the wiles of 'respectable' human nature, Peter
admonishes: 'Be hospitable to each other without secretly
wishing you hadn't got to be!' (v. 9, *JBP*). He knew that purity of motive
was more important than *doing* the expected thing. And this is the
emphasis he again makes in verse 11, which is concerned with
preaching *and* serving behind the scenes.

Christian activity so conveniently provides opportunities for the
unconscious parading of oneself; pride is then fed and the people to
whom one 'ministers' are silently humiliated.

Peter points to the only safeguard: we must see ourselves as
'stewards of the manifold grace of God' (v. 10, *KJV*). In the ancient
world, stewards were numerous. They acted on behalf of their
respective masters, knowing that none of the things over which they
had control belonged to themselves. Custodians of other people's
goods, they served only for their masters' benefit, never their own.
Any other motive left them open to easy temptation.

So Peter writes: ' One of you preaches, let him remember that it is
God's message he is uttering; another distributes relief, let him
remember that it is God who supplies him the opportunity; that so, in
all you do, God may be glorified through Jesus Christ' (v. 11, *RKT*).
That motive alone makes a Christian's service acceptable.

To ponder:
**'As long as a man remains the centre of his world, everything,
religion included, can be used in his service, to minister to his
own self-realisation, his own sense of dominion.'**
Bishop Stephen Neill

Easy Peace

....

'If a man suffers for being a Christian, he need not be ashamed,
he should rather glorify God for that' (v. 16, JMT).

The 'fiery trial' to which Peter refers did indeed burst upon these early believers. An explanation was sought for the fire of Rome, and Nero diverted suspicion away from himself by accusing the little-understood Christians. They were hunted like rats and, when caught, became the victims of the emperor's mad ravings.

Tacitus records the grim story:

They died in torments and their torments were embittered by insult and derision. Some were nailed on crosses, others sewn up in the skins of wild beasts and exposed to the fury of dogs; others again, smeared over with combustible materials, were used as torches to illuminate the darkness of the night.

Yet incredibly they died rejoicing. One of them greeted her violent end with, 'This is my coronation day.' Her spirit was typical. They were not 'ashamed' (v. 16, *KJV*) but counted themselves happy (v. 14) to be 'reproached for the name of Christ'. The secret? These ordinary men and women rejoiced, believing themselves to be 'partakers of Christ's sufferings' (v. 13). And such suffering, warned Peter, was inevitable – 'Think it not strange' (v. 12) – in the face of uncompromising witness.

Then what of our undisturbed peace? Have we allowed the world to squeeze us into its own mould, making us undistinguishable from the unbeliever? The absence of 'fiery trials' could indicate the presence of unfaithfulness. Let that thought search our hearts today.

Daily Preparedness

'Let those who by the will of God are suffering trust their souls to him, their faithful Creator, as they continue to do right' (v. 19, JMT).

Judgment must begin at the house of God, for the most privileged must always bear the greatest responsibility. This was something the people of Israel never fully learned; they allowed their 'election' by God to foster both national pride and bigoted contempt for all non-Jews. The apostle Peter here explains how believers, without morbid self-centredness, can prepare themselves for unavoidable judgment.

They should 'commit the keeping of their souls' to God (v. 19, *KJV*). This is a daily committal, as Leslie Tizard vividly realised during his final weeks of suffering from a fatal illness. He wrote:

It means to do that bit of my task which is within my power today, without worrying whether I shall be able to finish it, and leaving it in God's hands to make what use of it he can. It means bearing the day's suffering, if suffering there is to be, in the strength that the day brings, without worrying about how I shall endure the more severe trials that may come, but believing that 'as thy days, so shall thy strength be'.[15]

God is able to keep us from falling. So let's trust him to do it!

The believers should continue their 'well doing', translated by Phillips as 'go on doing all the good they can'. Those who live each day as though it were their last, cramming it simply with good deeds in the name of Christ, are ready always for judgment. Such people *do* good because they *are* good.

Characteristics of Service

'Carry out your charge as God would have it done, cordially, not like drudges, generously, not in the hope of sordid gain; not tyrannising, each in his own sphere, but setting an example' (vv. 2, 3, RKT).

In what spirit do we serve Christ? The answer is not necessarily obvious for, unhappily, the habits of years, though loyally maintained, can lose the essential spirit that initially fired them. In today's verses, the apostle focuses on four characteristics which, apart from outlining a minimum standard for the aspect of leadership under consideration, should mark every expression of Christian service.

We must serve willingly (v. 2). Few things are more contradictory than a half-hearted Christian. Yet how difficult it is to maintain enthusiasm and a willingness to serve in any capacity! Unless we are careful, we find ourselves doing only what we enjoy or cannot decently avoid.

We must serve the cause of Christ and not for personal gain (v. 2). When we – *our* interests and *our* wishes – become more important than the kingdom we profess to serve, our witness degenerates; and our selfishness is no less selfish because it has 'religious' associations.

We must serve with humility (v. 3). To minister to others without patronage, without making them feel small or embarrassed, or lording it over them, is possible only to the man or woman who remains at heart a slave of Christ.

We must serve as an example (v. 3). Before we complain about the indifference of our young people we should recognise that they are largely reflections of our own spirituality. Parents who are inconsistent in their religion cannot produce children filled with spiritual zeal; casual evangelical leaders cannot inspire enthusiastic evangelical followers. We must prayerfully ask ourselves whether our example is helping or hindering others in their search and service for God.

Humility

....

'Throw the whole of your anxiety upon him, because he himself cares for you' (v. 7, WNT).

In *Christian Holiness*, Stephen Neill recalls:

Over nearly forty years there comes back to me a beautiful description of a preacher returning from the University Church at Oxford with a bulky manuscript under his arm, bursting with pride because he had just preached so excellent a sermon on humility!

Well might Peter write: 'God resisteth the proud, and giveth grace to the humble. Humble yourselves therefore under the mighty hand of God' (vv. 5, 6, *KJV*).

Humility is not self-deprecation. To underestimate oneself is just as wrong as personal overestimation. Christian initiative and daring have been stifled far too often in the name of humility, falsely conceived. 'Self-confidence is essential, self-sufficiency is disastrous,' said E. J. Tinsley. 'Self-confidence means proper acceptance of ourselves as we are. Self-sufficiency is to persuade ourselves that we are what we can never be.'

Humility flows from honest self-knowledge. Shortly after a prominent citizen in Edinburgh had been imprisoned, and the whole city was scandalised, Dr Alexander Whyte walked into his vestry one Sunday morning as the bells were ringing for church. He turned to his assistant and said, 'Do you hear those bells? He hears them in his prison cell this morning. Man, it might have been me!' Such a person, a tower of strength to others, always feels the need to cast himself upon God's mercy; hence his strong serenity.

Finally, the holy kiss, a sign of respect and affection, was for centuries a part of Christian fellowship and worship. It was a customary greeting in the ancient world but, open to abuse, it gradually fell into disrepute. So let our final thought on this letter be centred upon Silvanus – almost certainly Silas, Paul's companion on some of his missionary travels. He is remembered primarily as the helper of men greater than himself. But their achievements were largely dependent on his loyalty.

How difficult it is to serve without getting the credit! Yet this is the very essence of Christian service, for its only motive is the glory of God. The believer has few harder lessons to learn.

A Distorted Picture

....

'Do nothing out of selfish ambition or vain conceit, but in humility consider others better than yourselves. Each of you should look not only to your own interests, but also to the interests of others' (vv. 3, 4).

William Booth, founder of The Salvation Army, once sent a one-word telegram to his leading officers around the world. It simply stated: 'Others'. Its meaning was unmistakable. Jesus had the same focus and demonstrated it clearly in his life as surely as he expounded it in his teaching. We should not live for ourselves alone – and we should always consider the possibility that looking at a problem purely from our own personal viewpoint can produce a distorted picture.

Viewpoint

I tend to get excited
When I can't get my own way,
Perhaps you heard the 'Hamlet'
I was playing yesterday!
My anger was quite
Justified.
You know I was provoked.
How dare they disagree
With me!
No wonder I was choked!

But when I come to look at things
Within the light of day,
I see them, you will understand,
In quite another way.
If I could turn the clock back
I'd sing quite another song.
The fact is, I'm ashamed to say,
I was completely wrong!

The Voice of a Countryman

The prophet Micah

Introduction

Micah prophesied at about the same time as Isaiah (the three kings of 1:1 ruled the southern kingdom of the Jews – Judah – from 750 to 687 BC). But whereas Isaiah was probably a prominent courtier, Micah had a peasant background. 'Pinched peasant faces peer between his words,' wrote Scottish theologian George Adam Smith.

Micah's warnings had added relevance in that the northern kingdom – Israel – fell to the Assyrians in 722 BC, while parts of Judah were captured and Jerusalem was in danger of being captured in 701 BC by the Assyrian king, Sennacherib.

These readings are from the pen of Major Clifford Kew and were first published in *The Soldier's Armoury* (forerunner of *Words of Life*) in July and August 1980.

For the Sunday readings, John Gowans continues to provide a prayer-poem with a selected Bible passage.

No Passing the Buck

....

'All this will happen because the people . . . have sinned and rebelled against God. Who is to blame? . . . Samaria, the capital city itself! Who is guilty? . . . Jerusalem itself!' (v. 5, GNB).

Today's reading is concerned with the judgment about to hit Judah: 'The Lord stands ready at Jerusalem's gates to punish her' (v. 9, *LB*). Verse 5 makes it plain where the blame lay for the impending doom. It lay with the people of Jerusalem themselves and their leaders, just as the fall of Samaria (722 BC) could be put down to its people. They could not make excuses and pass the buck, nor even blame the invading Assyrians. They had asked for all that was coming to them.

The American statesman Daniel Webster, asked for the most important thought he had ever entertained, replied, 'My individual responsibility to God.' The art of blame-shifting has been perfected in our day but the Christian can have no part of it.

Of course, the blame lay especially with the national leaders. It was in Samaria and Jerusalem that the canker proliferated. Yet no man is an island unto himself. He is part of a community, a body, and is either a healthy or a corrupting influence. Those in the corridors of power, those who make policy, have the greater responsibility for the community; but the Micahs, the peasants, are not excused from concern for the body's health. And the Christian does not opt out of public affairs.

Micah was not content to be a 'don't know', a 'floating voter' or a non-voter. He realised the personal responsibility of his people, his leaders, and himself for their communal plight, and sought to do something about it.

No Hiding Place

'The LORD will hand you over to an enemy, who is going to capture your town. The leaders of Israel will go and hide in the cave at Adullam' (v. 15, GNB).

When Tanzanian and Ugandan exile forces advanced into Uganda in 1979, the international press concentrated its interest almost exclusively on Entebbe Airport and the capital, Kampala. Little attention was given to the country areas and small towns which had to be overrun first. The strategic objectives monopolised the headlines.

In contrast, Micah here realises that those least defended and first to suffer in the coming Assyrian invasion will be the people of the countryside. He lists towns and villages on the western border with Philistia which the invaders will capture on the way to Jerusalem, including the village of Moresheth Gath, three miles from his own home. For their inhabitants, as the first half of verse 15 shows, there will be no hiding place.

Brother Andrew (in *Battle for Africa*) quotes an African nationalist leader who points out that there is more than one kind of discrimination: 'Not discrimination by . . . colonialists against Africans, but discrimination by Africans against Africans . . . by the "black suit" townsmen . . . by the educated men in power against their fellow countrymen.'

So Micah the countryman sees that the 'townies' will have the better of the situation to which their evil has made the greatest contribution. The 'glorious leaders' will have a way of escape, but even their hiding place will be a shameful 'cave at Adullam' (the limestone labyrinth where David and his outlaw army had hidden).

He who oppresses his weaker fellows may seem to have 'feathered his own nest', but that will be of little comfort to him when the scythe of history chops down the tree in which the nest is built.

A Cure for Pride

'You are going to find yourselves in trouble, and then you will not walk so proudly any more' (v. 3, GNB).

Having spoken of the poor countryman and of the political leaders of Judah, Micah now turns to unscrupulous businessmen and men of property; particularly to the exploiters of the poor, those who strip the poorer members of society of the few assets they do possess (vv. 1, 2).

To these Micah says, 'What is sauce for the goose is sauce for the gander.' Though they may have enjoyed immunity from prosecution in their own society, they will be hoist with their own petard when invasion comes (v. 4). And when the time comes for the Jews to re-establish themselves in the land, these 'sharks' will get nothing (v. 5).

In some ways adversity hits the prosperous harder than the poor. They have further to fall, and have been so insulated against hardship that, when they are left 'out in the cold', they have no resistance to the viruses of strife and deprivation.

Nevertheless adversity has its uses. The exploiters may be spiritually benefited by it. Pride goes before a fall but that may be no bad thing if the fall kills the pride.

The playwright Tennessee Williams had a long history of mental illness which included the continual fear that he was dying. He was severely depressed, his sister was in a mental hospital and he had unsatisfactory relationships with both his parents. But afterwards he said that without these experiences of misery, grief and despair he could never have written his plays.

To pray:
Help us, Lord, to see in adversity a rod to break the back of our pride, and a curriculum for the development of our character.

The False Prophet and the Good Shepherd

'The sort of prophet this people wants is a windbag and a liar,
prophesying a future of "wines and spirits"!' (v. 11, JBP).

'It can't be as bad as all that!' the opposition tells Micah (vv. 6, 7). 'God wouldn't treat us like that! We're too good for that!' Micah has little difficulty in dealing with that self-righteous claim: 'You would steal the "demob" suit off the back of an ex-serviceman' (v. 8). 'You evict widows and brainwash children out of their faith' (v. 9).

The true prophet often has to puncture the balloon of the sinner's self-righteousness. Joy Davidman in *Smoke on the Mountain* writes, 'The true prophet says humbly, "To me, a sinful man, God spoke." But the scribes and the Pharisees declare, "When we speak, God agrees . . ."'[16] It was truly 'the word of the LORD' that came to Micah (1:1, *NEB*) in contrast to the 'ranting' (2:6, *NEB*) of the insincere, 'professional' prophets.

Micah recognises (2:11) that it is the 'professional' who will be popular. The people want to hear 'smooth things'. 'They say, "Tell us what we want to hear. Let us keep our illusions"' (Isaiah 30:10, *GNB*). That way lies spiritual disaster.

Yet the true prophet sees a way back for his people; not a way back that avoids the inevitable disaster, but one in which 'the LORD himself' (Micah 2:13, *GNB*) will be the Good Shepherd leading those who will follow him into a fold which will be proof against the marauding 'wolves' who had previously savaged their communal peace.

> **Saviour, like a shepherd lead us,**
> **Much we need thy tender care;**
> **In thy pleasant pastures feed us,**
> **For our use thy folds prepare.**
> *Dorothy Ann Thrupp*

The Sun Goes Down

....

*'But as for me, the LORD fills me with his spirit and power,
and gives me a sense of justice and the courage to tell the people of
Israel what their sins are' (v. 8, GNB).*

In chapter 3 Micah continues his unmasking of Judah's prophets and leaders: 'Your day is almost over; the sun is going down on you' (v. 6). Cross their palm with silver and you would get a good horoscope (v. 5); but because they misled people, they would lose the tools of their trade – vision and the ability to predict (v. 6). And the future would prove them wrong (v. 7).

In our age of 'scientific reason', it is amazing that so many lend gullible ears to those who predict the future; and yet perhaps understandable, for 'We are all interested in the future, for the future is where we will spend the rest of our lives.' We may be so fascinated that we fail to notice how often 'those who predict the future' are 'disgraced by their failure' (v. 7). In any case, 'What better fortune could a person have than the one promised to all believers in Jesus Christ?' (Gary Wilburn).

In contrast, Micah does not use the things of God for personal profit, but allows God to use him as his tool. He is indwelt by God's Spirit and energised by his power. He discerns the truth by a God-given sense of justice, and he is given the courage to apply it without fear or favour in his own situation (v. 8).

Benjamin Jowett writes: 'The prophet lives with God rather than with his fellow-men; and he is confident that the word which he speaks is the Word of God.'

Where Money Talks

'The city's rulers govern for bribes, the priests interpret the Law for pay, the prophets give their revelations for money – and they all claim that the LORD is with them. "No harm will come to us," they say. "The LORD is with us"' (v. 11, GNB).

In these verses Micah makes a summary of his analysis of social evil, before introducing a new subject in the next chapter. It would seem that the trouble all boiled down to money.

In itself money is neither good nor bad but morally neutral. It can be like another pair of hands. It can oil the wheels of society in the nicest possible way. But Micah is talking of tainted money, though those who handle it would no doubt justify their methods on some ground or other. As Francis Bacon wrote, 'Money is like muck, not good except it be spread.' So it is the 'love of money' that is 'the root of all evil'.

In verse 11 all three groups to whom an Israelite in trouble could turn are shown to be corrupt – the city rulers, the priests and the prophets. We may rejoice that in some modern societies medical and legal aid are no longer completely governed by purse and wallet, but it may still be true in other respects that, 'In a day when almost every service has a price tag, there is real danger that qualities such as justice and truth and the nobility of disinterested public service may be lost to the community altogether' (J. H. Gailey). Such a spirit may even infect the religious who 'claim that the LORD is with them' (v. 11).

What is needed is the type of leader of whom it may be said, as Pope Pius IV said of John Calvin, that his power 'lay in the fact that he was indifferent to money'. He was not for sale.

Be Grateful

....

*'Do everything without complaining or arguing, so that you may
become blameless and pure, children of God without fault in
a crooked and depraved generation, in which you shine like
stars in the universe' (vv. 14, 15).*

If only we could always be what we are in our best moments! Why do
we so easily give in to petty temptations such as the desire to
bemoan our lot? Is it because we see them as petty, so it doesn't really
matter? But if we really are to shine 'like stars in the universe', our
complaints and arguments are going to have to go. They're unworthy
of God's creation. And we'll feel better without them!

Irritants

I'm sorry that
I moan so much
And for no reason.
The smallest irritation,
Off I go!
I get the better
Of my groans
But for a season,
Then back they swarm again.
It's wrong I know.
It's such a stupid habit,
Willy-nilly
Complaining's second nature,
And so silly.

Don't take my grousing
Seriously,
Forgive me freely.
I've got so many blessings and
I'm grateful
Really!

A Better Tomorrow

'Each man shall dwell under his own vine, under his own fig-tree, undisturbed' (v. 4, NEB).

Chapter 4 brings a complete change of subject, and is perhaps by another prophet in a later generation. One contrast is that in the previous verses Micah puts all Israel's problems down to corrupt human leadership, while here the writer sees hope for the future in a divine takeover. It is 'the Lord' who brings about the transformation. One writer says, 'As Christians we may be short-term pessimists but . . . long-term optimists: in the short term confusion and evil run riot . . . in the long term God reigns.'

So a Jew in Auschwitz could scrawl on a wall: 'I believe in the sun even when it is not shining. I believe in love even when I·cannot feel it. I believe in God even when he is silent'; and Corrie ten Boom could write (in *The Hiding Place*) of Ravensbruck, another concentration camp: 'We sat by deathbeds that became doorways of heaven. We watched women who had lost everything grow rich in hope.'[17]

If it be true (as Denis Duncan says) that 'peace is love resting', then Micah sees it as resting against a rural background. Sitting under one's own vine and fig-tree was a proverbial concept of peace and prosperity (see 1 Kings 4:25; Isaiah 36:16; Zechariah 3:10).

The vision is, of course, still far from being realised. A *British Weekly* comment column stated: 'Jesus must be weeping that, two millennia after he wept over Jerusalem, we still don't know the things that make for peace.'

The Paradox of Affliction

'I will make the disabled the stock of the future, and a strong nation of those who are sick' (v. 7, JBP).

In verses 6 and 7 terms vary greatly in the different translations, but all give a clear picture of the triumph of the underdog – the crippled, the outcast, the afflicted, the disabled, the sick (*JBP*); the lame, the cast off (*RSV*); the lost, the exiles, the weaklings, the derelict (*NEB*); the dispossessed (*LB*) – these are the raw materials of the coming kingdom.

It is not the way of the world to start from 'a position of weakness', but all the forms of weakness mentioned above apply to physical disability rather than spiritual. Might it not be true that the underdog may have more leisure from the demands of self in which to develop more spiritual muscle than the he-man and the man of means?

Actor Raymond Burr (TV detective Perry Mason) suffered blow after blow. His first wife died in a plane crash. His only son died at the age of ten of leukaemia. His second marriage broke down and his third wife died of cancer. Yet he said: 'When something untoward happens, you have to develop a larger insight into life just to continue living properly.'

The gloating invaders 'do not know the thoughts of the LORD, nor do they understand his plan' (4:12). God's best garment will be made from a remnant. He 'moves in a mysterious way . . . Deep in unfathomable mines of never-failing skill, he treasures up his bright designs' (William Cowper). Those who allow their lives to be programmed by God will be 'as strong as a bull with iron horns and bronze hoofs' (4:13, *GNB*).

The Backwater Messiah

'He shall appear and be their shepherd in the strength of the LORD, *in the majesty of the name of the* LORD *his God . . . and he shall be a man of peace' (vv. 4, 5, NEB).*

In chapter 4 the prophet was referring to 'the LORD' (Jehovah), but in 5:1 he writes of a human 'leader of Israel', one born of woman (v. 3). However, he clearly sees him in quite unexpected terms, in direct contrast to existing leadership.

This Messiah (for these verses are used of Jesus in Matthew 2:6 and John 7:42) will come from a 'backwater' village 'almost too small to be counted' (v. 2, JBP); yet he is the inheritor of all Israel's history; his 'roots are far back in the past, in days gone by' (v. 2). His strength and majesty will be spiritual (v. 4), and he will function as a shepherd (v. 4, NEB) rather than as a military leader. 'People all over the earth will acknowledge his greatness' (v. 4, GNB) and finally 'He shall be a man of peace' (v. 5, NEB).

Yet this deliverance is not yet. In verse 3 Micah suggests that his coming will be associated with the nation's return from exile, but the earlier part of the verse has the vaguer phrase 'until his mother gives birth to him' (JMT). Until then the Lord will 'leave them to themselves'.

To be abandoned by God to the results of one's own sinfulness is a fearful thing, like a child rebellious against parental authority yet devastated when his parents are killed in a road crash. We don't expect God to take us seriously, to leave us to our own devices. But he might just do that if he can't get through to us.

Sweet Influence

••

'The people of Israel who survive will be like refreshing dew
sent by the LORD for many nations, like showers on growing plants.
They will depend on God, not human beings' (v. 7, GNB).

Our text suggests that the remnant of the Jews will by dispersion have a good but relentless influence on other nations. This will apply, however, only to the 'survivors' of the great disaster and exile which is to oppress the whole nation (v. 7).

Verses 8 and 9 seem to express an attitude contradictory to that found in verses 7 and 10–14. Adversity can have two effects on people, depending on their own reaction to it. It can make them bitter or it can make them a 'sweet influence'.

Viktor E. Frankl, in his preface to *The Unconscious God*, writes: 'A weak faith is weakened by predicaments and catastrophes whereas a strong faith is strengthened by them.'[18] A woman Salvationist witnessed: 'At the all-time low of my life God put some steel into my spiritual experience.' And a gardener applies the same principles: 'If you want a good rose, sharpen your knife and harden your heart.' The 'sweet influence' of the Christian is often strongest when God has pruned him back hard.

It is also often necessary for God to knock away the 'props' on which we have come to depend, so that we 'will depend on God, not human beings' (v. 7). In verses 10–14 Micah lists many props which sustained the Jews – cavalry, chariots, cities, defences, magic, fortune-telling and idolatry of various kinds. We might add nuclear stockpiling and, at the other extreme, fascination with the occult. If we have come to rely on such props we are liable to fall flat on our faces when the props are removed.

What God Wants

··

'What does the LORD require of you but to do justice, and to love kindness, and to walk humbly with your God?' (v. 8, RSV).

This, the best known verse in Micah, gives one of the simplest yet most comprehensive definitions of the godly life. The previous verses call the Israelites to remember all that God has done for them, and to realise how far they are from him now. They've got it all wrong! They've forgotten what God wants, so much so that they go on with their religious duties unaware that those observances are of no avail because they are neglecting the basic essentials of spiritual life – justice, love and humility.

The mechanical observance of religious duty without reference to basic principles may eventually lead to a Christian finding himself in absurd and contradictory situations. He has forgotten 'what it's all about', like the boy who touched every lamp post on his way home from school because 'he felt guilty if he didn't do it'. Religion based on unthinking habits can be exacting yet unsatisfying.

It is only by reference to basic principles such as those given in verse 8 that an understanding of God's will can be reached, and religious duties held in balance. Those who provided the animals used in temple sacrifices, at great profit to themselves, were condemned because their 'religious' activity lacked justice. The priest and Levite going to carry out their temple duty were condemned because their ignoring of the robbers' victim showed a lack of love. The Pharisee praying next to a quisling tax collector was condemned because his prayer lacked humility. They had neglected the basic essentials.

And the qualities essential in the individual must also be the foundations on which a Christian community is built.

The Counter-productiveness of Materialism

••

'You will eat but never have enough . . . And though you try and try to save your money . . . what little you succeed in storing up I'll give to those who conquer you!' (v. 14, LB).

Thomas Carlyle said of the economist Bentham, 'He thinks he can rebuild society by the simple maxim that food is pleasant in the belly and money in the purse. He cannot. He can destroy it.' And when Rockefeller was asked, 'How much wealth does it take to satisfy a man?' he replied, 'Just a little more.' Material acquisitiveness cannot guarantee spiritual satisfaction. In fact excessive indulgence may bring about even physical dissatisfaction.

The materialist fails to recognise that we are not guaranteed that our life's span will be long enough for us to achieve our materialistic goals (Luke 12:20). In fact the opposite is true, for the materialist is never satisfied. It is always a case of 'just a little more'.

In contrast, the attractiveness of justice, love and humility (Micah 6:8) never palls. You can never have too much of the genuine article, but every little sample of it brings intense satisfaction. True religion is never boring.

A book review in *British Weekly* spoke of 'a whole generation of young people who are being bored to death in the name of the least boring man in history, Jesus Christ, whom people either adored or sought to crucify'; and of 'good and earnest people who have turned the explosive challenge and adventure of the Christian gospel into the most boring subject in the school curriculum'. It is not the gospel that is boring but its presentation.

The well of living water springing up in everlasting freshness contrasts markedly with the staleness of physical 'satisfactions'.

Let Go

....

'Whatever is true, whatever is noble, whatever is right, whatever is pure, whatever is lovely, whatever is admirable – if anything is excellent or praiseworthy – think about such things' (v. 8).

The apostle Paul hit it right on the nail when he wrote about us humans often finding ourselves doing what we don't want to do. Deep down, we want to do the right thing, but our humanity pulls us in the wrong direction – like iron filings irresistibly drawn to a powerful magnet. Except evil need not be irresistible. We each decide what thoughts settle in our mind, and God's grace is stronger than our strongest 'natural' urge.

Hurts

I'm glad I can forget
All kinds of things,
Life's hurts and harms,
Its unexpected stings.
I contemplate
My bruises for a while
And then I let them go again
And smile!

But when I nurse
Some special wound or woe,
And stubbornly
Refuse to let it go,
Prise from my fingers
What might fester there.
And cleanse my mem'ry
Of encrusting care.

It may prove rather painful
But I'll be
A cleaner, saner, sounder,
Nobler me!

The Breakdown of Society

> 'But I will watch for the LORD; I will wait confidently for God,
> who will save me. My God will hear me' (v. 7, GNB).

Here Micah gives a vivid but pessimistic picture of the breakdown of Jewish society. He likens it (v. 1) to a harvested vineyard or orchard where no useful fruit is left, but only rotten fruit littering the ground.

From a human point of view the situation is totally hopeless. There has been a breakdown in goodness (v. 1); in honesty (v. 2); in religion (v. 2); in law and order (v. 2); in justice and administration (v. 3); in friendship (v. 5); even in husband-and-wife relationships (see v. 5); and in family life where the generation gap is seen at its worst (v. 6). And those who perpetrate such social evils, do so most energetically (v. 3).

So Micah looks at the scene with no hope for society. It is a quagmire of futilities. Corruption has taken such a hold that no one man's efforts can alter the situation. He does the one thing he can do – he watches and prays. He trusts God for personal salvation, but also he knows that God has the answer to the ills of society. He is a short-term pessimist, but a long-term optimist (note that despair can be a thing of the moment, or it can be a way of life).

When the Scottish Reformation army had been repulsed and there was general gloom, John Knox mounted the pulpit and cried, 'It is the eternal truth of the eternal God that we maintain; it may be oppressed for a time, but in the end it will surely triumph.' Such habitual trust in God is necessary if the Christian is to keep his faith in the midst of a 'perverse and foolish generation'.

A Tide in the Affairs of Men

••

'When I fall, I shall rise again; when I sit in darkness, the LORD shall be my light' (v. 8, JBP).

Micah believes that the tide will turn, that eventually God's purposes for Judah will raise her from her downcast state. The enemies who are 'gloating' over the Jews, will eventually be 'trampled down like mud in the streets' (v. 10, *GNB*). A similar hope of survival in the midst of trials is often found in the New Testament (for example in 2 Corinthians 4:7–9).

Micah acknowledges that his people's predicament is largely of their own making (v. 9) and that the maintenance of a moral universe demands that, for a time at least, they should suffer the consequences of their own sin. The only way towards a more blessed future is the acknowledgement of sin and a willingness to have it dealt with.

Paul Tournier writes in *Guilt and Grace*:

The only true solution [to guilt] both from the psychological standpoint and in the light of the Bible, is . . . the acceptance of our responsibilities, genuine recognition of our guilt and repentance, and the receiving of God's forgiveness in response to this repentance.[19]

Restoration is coming, therefore (vv. 11, 12). There will be a return of scattered Jews from east (Mesopotamia) and west (Egypt). The city walls will be rebuilt and the kingdom enlarged. Yet in verse 13 there is still a suggestion of nature 'getting its own back' on man. The spiritual truth is that the consequences of sin often cannot be avoided even when it is forgiven.

The way people treat their world may very well determine how the world treats them.

Buried in the Deepest Sea

··

'There is no other god like you, O LORD; you forgive the sins of your people who have survived. You do not stay angry for ever, but you take pleasure in showing us your constant love' (v. 18, GNB).

An old Salvation Army chorus runs:

> Gone, gone, gone, gone, all my sins are gone . . .
> Buried in the deepest sea,
> That is good enough for me.

In the triumphant climax of this book, Micah tells God that there is no one like him for forgiving (v. 18), for shepherding his people (v. 14), for working miracles (v. 15), for keeping his promises (v. 20). He is unique (v. 18). And whereas in verse 10 Micah was preoccupied with the 'trampling down' of his enemies, now his first concern is for the 'trampling underfoot' of his own sins (v. 19).

Martin Luther said: 'If the world had treated me like it has treated God, I would long ago have kicked the wretched thing to pieces.' But God is unique in his willingness to forgive. It is because of the inner security we have in knowing such a God that we can 'trust where we cannot trace'.

Mrs Albert Einstein was asked if she understood the theory of relativity propounded by her husband. 'No,' was her reply, 'but I know my husband, and I know he can be trusted.' A close friend of someone accused of serious crime may say, 'I know him too well. I know he couldn't do such a thing.'

It is this kind of personal relationship which inspired trust in God on Micah's part, and which can do the same for us.

··

> The storm may roar without me,
> My heart may low be laid;
> But God is round about me,
> And can I be dismayed?
> *Anna L. Waring*

That's Life

....

Readings from the book of Proverbs

Introduction

Proverbs of the non-religious kind are part of the background of our thinking. Similarly, the book of Proverbs is part of the background of Hebrew thought which produced the Old Testament. It is folklore rather than philosophy, and some of it is queried elsewhere in the Bible, for instance in the book of Job.

It is repetitive poetry of a particular kind, based on current ideas of Wisdom in Old Testament times. It has much in common with other ancient Wisdom literature, from such places as Egypt, Babylon and Syria. It is the product of many minds, though specific sections are attributed to Solomon, Agur and Lemuel. The passages chosen for comment are mostly those having some relation to the New Testament.

These readings are from the pen of Major David Dalziel and were first published in *The Soldier's Armoury* (forerunner of *Words of Life*) in September and October 1988.

For the Sunday readings, John Gowans continues to provide a prayer-poem with a selected Bible passage.

Wealth, Women or Wisdom?

'The proverbs of Solomon, son of David and king of Israel . . .
These proverbs can even add to the knowledge of wise men and
give guidance to the educated' (vv. 1, 5, GNB).

Which is Solomon remembered for – his wealth, his women or his wisdom? Jesus mentions Solomon's glory – his wealth – but immediately brings us down to earth, saying it cannot compare even with the adornment of a simple lily in a field (Luke 12:27). He also speaks of Solomon's wisdom, saying it is nothing compared with his own (Matthew 12:42). The New Testament ignores the women, but 1 Kings leaves us in no doubt that Solomon was lured away from God by them (11:4).

We are left with a problem which takes every ounce of wisdom to contemplate. Can we accept as truly wise a man who thought wisely but acted foolishly? His political actions, too, left much to be desired. He forced centralised government on people not yet ready for it (1 Kings 4:19), used forced labour (1 Kings 5:13) and left his son a bad example (1 Kings 12:11). Jesus again comes to our rescue as he says of the authorities, 'You must obey and follow everything they tell you to do; do not, however, imitate their actions, because they don't practise what they preach' (Matthew 23:3, GNB).

Such simple advice sounds easy, but it isn't. We naturally follow those whom we like or admire. It also opens up possibilities for those who glory in saying, 'Don't do as I do, do as I say.'

As we study the book of Proverbs, may we take from it the ancient wisdom, without prejudice; apply our critical faculty to it; and go beyond Old Testament wisdom into the New, just as Jesus did when he said, 'You have heard that people were told in the past . . . but now I tell you . . .' (Matthew 5:21, 22, GNB).

Adam's Sin

....

'To have knowledge, you must first have reverence for the LORD. Stupid people have no respect for wisdom and refuse to learn' (v. 7, GNB).

Adam's sin was to seek for knowledge without reverence for the Lord. He thought that by knowing he would become equal to his maker: 'You will be like God' (Genesis 3:5). Knowledge used without reverence for, or reference to, God is dangerous.

Discovery of the structure of the atom is probably the most sensational example. Most of those working in the field of atomic physics are ordinary people, no better, no worse than the rest of us. But if their knowledge was used without reference to an ethical code, above and beyond the discoveries they make, disaster would result.

Genetic engineering is potentially an even more explosive problem than the atom bomb. The possibilities are infinite, and those with the skill to manipulate conditions of life in the womb, or even more remarkably in a test tube, can easily feel they are 'playing God'. Without a humble sense of dependence on God for that knowledge, and without strong ethical codes which are very difficult to formulate, the potential for disaster is enormous.

In response to such problems many of us feel the only thing we can do is ignore them and hope the worst won't happen. But that is exactly the way of the 'stupid' person so roundly condemned in verse 32.

We cannot be condemned for having less academic ability than the atomic scientist or the genetic engineer. Our skills may be quite different, but we are all condemned if we do not make our voices heard in support of the wisdom of the Lord, a wisdom which includes reverence for God, for life itself and for the environment in which life is lived.

Robbery

• •

'Robbery always claims the life of the robber – this is what
happens to anyone who lives by violence' (v. 19, GNB).

Robin Hood robbed the rich to give to the poor. He has been idolised
by many adults as well as by young people fed on a diet of fantasy
and adventure. Some time ago, in London, supposedly the most secure
safe deposit in the world was robbed of millions of pounds' worth of
jewels. The operation was undertaken so successfully, so slickly and
without injury to anyone that many people expressed a sneaking – or
even open – admiration for the Robin Hood-type figures who stole
from the rich.

A few days before that, in the poorer end of the same city, two
robbers with guns were shot dead by police as they carried out a raid.
No admiration was expressed for those men. The press comment was
almost entirely that 'they got what they deserved', though the families
of the men sprang to their defence.

But the successful, admired criminals were also armed, and actually
held a gun to someone's head. They were just as much taken over by
violence. The only differences were their sensational target, and the
fact that their capture took longer. Their lives were claimed as surely
as those of the criminals who were shot dead. Their assumption that
violence pays was reinforced, making it harder for them to turn away
from violence than before their 'successful' raid and making it more
likely that they would threaten others in future.

That was small comfort to the families of those shot dead in the
course of robbery, but it should give us all cause to think when the
violent seem to get things all their own way.

Frequent Praying

••

'Do not be anxious about anything, but in everything, by prayer and petition, with thanksgiving, present your requests to God. And the peace of God, which transcends all understanding, will guard your hearts and your minds in Christ Jesus' (vv. 6, 7).

We really should not be confused about how to pray. The Bible offers us plenty of advice. Not least, it encourages us to practise it often. God will never tire of hearing our voices raised in prayer to him – even if we do say the same thing time and again. If it's on our heart and mind, then it should be on our lips in prayer. And there will be a reward: peace, of a kind that 'transcends all understanding'.

Renewal

My praying has
A too-familiar ring,
And you must sigh
To hear the same old thing.
My worn complaints,
The silly same excuse –
Do you get tired
And wonder what's the use
Of picking up
The broken pieces, Lord,
And starting me afresh?
You must get bored!

Perhaps not,
And the truth is
That you'd rather
Your children
Brought their bruises
To their Father!

75

Watch Out! Wisdom is Calling!

'Listen! Wisdom is calling out in the streets and market places . . .
Foolish people! How long do you want to be foolish? . . . You have
ignored all my advice and have not been willing to let me correct
you. So when you get into trouble I will laugh at you'
(vv. 20, 22, 25, 26, GNB).

Wisdom is portrayed as personal in the book of Proverbs. She speaks (v. 20). She laughs and jeers (v. 26). She protects (v. 33). She makes plans (8:14). She loves (8:17). And she was born, the first of all creation (8:22). This last statement will be considered later. Today our concern is for the character of Wisdom.

In many respects she is portrayed in a similar way to the way Jesus is described in the New Testament. She is deeply moved (v. 22), very like Jesus when he looked over Jerusalem and wept (Luke 19:41, 42). She longs to bring everyone within the fold of her protection and security, in similar fashion to Jesus, wanting to find the lost sheep and bring it home (Luke 15:4ff).

But there is also a great difference. When people reject Wisdom she laughs. She mocks them in a way quite foreign to the New Testament. When men finally turn to her she rejects them, unlike the Saviour who requires us to: 'Keep on asking . . . keep on seeking . . . keep on knocking' (Luke 11:9, WB).

Wisdom, then, is not something we can pick up any time we please. If we go on ignoring, if we persist in despising, we shall find that Wisdom eludes us. Similarly, by seeking Wisdom herself rather than God, the source of Wisdom, we risk being met with hollow laughter, mocking when terror strikes.

Cultural Relevance

....

'Never let go of loyalty and faithfulness' (v. 3, GNB).

What's sauce for the goose is sauce for the gander. The cultural background of Proverbs comes through strongly here. Faced with the powerful forces of sexual desire, and the woefully common fact of infidelity, a male-dominated society tended, as it often still does, to lay blame at the door of the woman.

Instead of reckoning with man's predatory instincts, and the need for him to control his behaviour, the writer of this section can only think that the woman who charms her lover is to blame. So an incomplete picture is given. The same thing also needs saying the other way round. Substitute 'she' for 'he' and vice versa throughout 2:16–22 and the picture will be complete.

The advice as it stands, though sexist by modern standards, is still good. In recent years, unfortunately, a new, practical impetus has been given, in the form of AIDS, to the age-old advice to 'just say no'. But even that is not sufficient to alter the behaviour of many who have been brought up to think sexual gratification is a right, on a par with food and shelter, and that any request for control of one's behaviour is kill-joy.

Even the word 'morality' when it refers to sexual morality is used as a form of abuse. How often we hear people saying apologetically 'I'm not moralising', as though morals were something to be ashamed of!

....

To pray:
We confess, Lord, it is often hard to be loyal. Blaming another person for our own shortcomings is so easy. Sometimes those we have promised to love and cherish appear not to return that love. Give us grace to persevere with difficult relationships, and where that is not possible, give us the ability to withdraw without bitterness or rancour.

Procrastination

....

*'Remember the LORD in everything you do and he will show you
the right way . . . Never tell your neighbours to wait until tomorrow
if you can help them now' (vv. 6, 28, GNB).*

Procrastination is the thief of time, and time-saving is a modern
disease. Household appliances, computers, cars, office equipment
– the list of things which aim to save us time is endless.

But what do we do with the time saved? Sometimes we simply rush
about even more than before. The beach that was inaccessible a
generation ago now beckons as a day trip by car rather than the goal
of a long-awaited holiday. Clothes changed weekly by older generations are now changed daily, thanks to the availability of washing
machines. We live further from our places of work, so take longer
travelling. We sit longer at our 'time-saving' machines, then need to
spend time jogging to compensate.

There are, however, positive ways of using time. When the odd ten
minutes comes along, remember your neighbour who is lonely. Time
spent listening in such circumstances is not wasted. In a more practical
vein, are your hedge-cutters more effective than those used by your
elderly neighbour? Use the time saved on your own hedge to do
someone else's.

Such advice may not sound like deep theology but it is the theology
of Jesus. Let's sense our neighbour's need and act upon it. 'In all thy
ways acknowledge him, and he shall direct thy paths' (v. 6, *KJV*).

Worldly-wise

'Don't let yourself go to sleep or even stop to rest. Get out of the trap like a bird or a deer escaping from a hunter' (vv. 4, 5, GNB).

Much of this book of Proverbs gives an impression of unworldly simplicity or naivety. Simply pleading for release from a debt (v. 3) doesn't work in a modern world where professional debt collectors lean heavily on poor people who can't afford to pay back the money they have borrowed at extortionate interest, any more than it worked in Jesus' day – as witness his story of one who was forgiven a large debt but tried to force a lesser debtor to pay up (Matthew 18:24–30).

Those on the debt spiral, whatever caused it in the first place, need our sympathy – and often more than a little help.

But when we reach verses 4 and 5, a very different picture emerges. What started as a naive, simplistic comment turns out to be made in full knowledge of the difficulties. It is as hard to wriggle out of responsibilities as it is for a bird or an animal to release itself from a trap.

Our only hope lies in making the effort: in proverbial language 'grasping the nettle'. The worst thing we can do is ignore the problem, hoping it will go away.

Tender-handed stroke a nettle
And it stings you for your pains;
Grasp it like a man of mettle
And it soft as silk remains.
Aaron Hill (1685–1750)

A Hymn to Wisdom

'I was there when he set the sky in place . . . I was there when
he laid the earth's foundations. I was beside him like an architect'
(vv. 27, 29, 30, GNB).

This passage should be compared with John 1:1–14, Colossians 1:15–18 and Revelation 3:14. The description of Wisdom in this chapter struck a chord with New Testament writers who felt it described just how they experienced Jesus.

The prologue of John's Gospel, which some people think of as a piece of semi-Greek philosophy, is seen to be rooted firmly in Hebrew Old Testament tradition when compared with this passage. Substitute 'Word' for 'Wisdom' and you could almost – but not quite – slot this passage into John's Gospel.

Like Wisdom, so Christ, the Word of Life, has always existed. Christ played his part in Creation as architect, right-hand man to God himself. But in a footnote to the hymn to Wisdom it gives 'a little child' as an alternative to 'architect'. The text is obscure but a similar word in Lamentations 4:4 means 'child'.

How appropriate! The architect of all creation is also a child. Surely there is a lesson for architects here, to act in humility; to view their grandiose schemes through the eyes of a child. To the rest of us it brings home yet again the simplicity of the gospel; the need for child-like faith; and the wonder of God using a child in Creation, as well as in saving humanity.

SATURDAY 15 NOVEMBER   PROVERBS 9:1–17

Opposite Attractions

• •

*'Wisdom: "Come, eat my food and drink the wine that
I have mixed" . . . Folly: "Stolen water is sweeter. Stolen bread
tastes better"' (vv. 5, 17, GNB).*

There is no denying that folly can be fun. If it weren't, fewer people
would go along her path. The same imagery of seduction is used
here as in chapters 5 and 7.

In practical terms, the fun of folly needs setting against its long-term
consequences. One basic difference between men and animals is a
conscious ability to sacrifice short-term advantage in favour of long-
term gain. This is easy to see in the realm of sexual relations. A
moment's pleasure may lead to lifelong disaster. Many recognise this,
and moderate their behaviour accordingly. Others take the risk. Some
'get away with it'. Some don't.

The thrill of risk-taking cannot be denied either. Gambling, sport,
fast cars, motor bikes, business, politics – even visiting new places,
meeting new friends – all can get the adrenalin flowing and give a
feeling of elation.

It seems then that following Wisdom involves denying ourselves all
the fun in life! Happily, however, Wisdom has its attractions too. There
is just as much risk involved in denying yourself to follow Jesus as in
the most thrilling of adventures. The food and drink of Wisdom is
indeed exciting, but takes a little longer to appreciate than some of the
momentary excitement of a passing pleasure.

As John Newton, the converted slave trader, put it in one of his
hymns:

Solid joys and lasting treasure
None but Zion's children know.

81

Mean It

....

'If you think you are standing firm, be careful that you don't fall!' (v. 12).

Steadfastness and consistency are admirable qualities. Stubbornness and a blinkered view are not. And a grudging apology is worthless. Note the joined-up word at the end of that sentence. An insincere apology is not just worth less than a heartfelt one . . . it is literally worthless. God is not fooled, even if others are. Let's try to do better.

Apology

You told me to say 'sorry'
So I did.
You can't say
That I don't do
As I'm bid!
You should have seen the way
His eyes met mine –
I told you it would be
A waste of time.
He's not the kind,
When all is said and done,
I ought to waste
My finer feelings on!

You wish I hadn't bothered,
Did I hear?
I've only gone
And made things worse,
You fear?
If I can't feel repentant
When I should
Then saying sorry
Isn't any good?

I'll try again.
I'll do it straight away.
O help me, Lord,
To mean the things I say!

Short Sayings

••

*'Intelligent people talk sense, but stupid people need to be
punished . . . Wealth protects the rich; poverty destroys the poor.
The reward for doing good is life, but sin leads only to more sin'*
(vv. 13, 15, 16, GNB).

Chapter 10 is the start of a section of short sayings, each of which
could be the subject of a whole article. The writer flits from one
thought to another. Sometimes there is a connection from one verse to
the next. Occasionally there is a series of related verses, but more often
each verse stands on its own.

Some read very strangely, for example verse 13, which says stupid
people need punishment. To interpret that, we need to remember that
'stupidity' in Proverbs means something more than a mere lack of
brain power.

Other sayings are more straightforward, though they often carry
more truth than is immediately obvious. For example: 'Wealth protects
the rich; poverty destroys the poor.' Simple, yet profound. Wealth does
indeed cushion the rich and cut them off from the realities of life.
Poverty ensnares the poor, feeding on itself all the time to make them
poorer. Volumes could be written on that one theme alone.

Some proverbs speak more truly than they know, as in verse 16. To
the writer of Proverbs, life is simply life here on earth, and his message
is therefore 'Be good and live long.' But we know differently. Jesus has
made us aware of a life beyond the grave, which is the goal of our own
short existence on earth. It is that goal to which goodness aspires.

Sin separates us from it. The only end of sin is more sin, then finally
destruction. Salvation means just that – being saved from the
destruction wrought by sin.

Economic Realities

· ·

*'People curse someone who hoards grain, waiting for a higher price,
but they praise the one who puts it up for sale' (v. 26, GNB).*

Economic realities have a strong effect on the Old Testament. Greed,
envy, exploitation, even inflation are found in its pages. These few
verses in chapter 11 make a number of points about money and the use
of money. Even verse 22 probably has an economic reference, for a
woman's judgment was brought into play most strongly in the
management of household finances (see also 14:1).

It is clear that the writer does not go as far as 1 Timothy 6:10, which
claims 'the love of money is the root of all evil'. But he does see it as
the source of some kinds of evil. It gives people power over others, and
anything which gives power can be misused. Grain gives power. Those
who control its distribution can make life-or-death decisions on behalf
of their fellows. Christians should pray for the enlightenment of those
in authority who wield such power through the distribution or
withholding of resources.

On a personal level we cannot expect others to act in a generous
spirit of concern for the needy if we hoard our own personal resources.
Lines from Annie Johnson Flint's hymn are relevant here:

> For out of his infinite riches in Jesus
> He giveth and giveth and giveth again.

Written to describe God's grace, these words are not blasphemous
when applied as a standard for the individual Christian. We each have
resources, spiritual and material, which are best used in giving to
others.

Punishment

....

'Don't hesitate to discipline children . . . it may save their lives'
(vv. 13, 14, GNB).

Many people are happy that corporal punishment has been
outlawed in a number of countries, including the United
Kingdom. Children may no longer be punished physically in schools,
or slapped – however lightly – by anyone, including their parents.
Other people, however, are unhappy – and some quote Bible texts like
this one, even though they were written thousands of years ago in very
different circumstances. If it's good enough for the book of Proverbs,
they say, it's good enough for us! But we have already noted the
corrupting influence of money, and the tendency to misuse it. Physical
punishment is surely similar. Give it full rein and it will take over.

It may be true that chastising children as the book of Proverbs
suggests will not kill the children, and might indeed make them think
before repeating whatever incurred the punishment, but the
temptation is always there to go one step further. Even if one moment
of physical abuse – for that, surely, is what such punishment is – has
what seems to be a positive effect, it does not mean that such action is
always effective. Indeed, it is more likely to begin a cycle of violence
which is impossible to stop. The child becomes used to the moment of
pain and it no longer serves as a warning.

Another possible consequence is that the child becomes the butt of
the anger of a parent or teacher.

....

To ponder:
Discipline means teaching, not punishment.

True Neighbourliness

....

'Singing to a person who is depressed is like taking off his clothes on a cold day or like rubbing salt in a wound. If your enemies are hungry, feed them; if they are thirsty, give them a drink. You will make them burn with shame, and the LORD will reward you' (vv. 20–22, GNB).

We have all met the person who is so cheerful that everyone else can hardly bear it! Some people find it impossible to 'weep with those who weep' (Romans 12:15) and hard to refrain from 'singing to a person who is depressed' (v. 20). Verse 17 applies particularly to them!

But sometimes singing to the depressed can be effective. And although salt in a wound (v. 20) is painful it can also be cleansing. Treat your enemy well (vv. 21, 22). It will make him uncomfortable but how it can cleanse! It stands a chance of breaking the cycle of violence.

Albert Schweitzer wrote:

All ordinary violence produces its own limitations, for it calls forth an answering violence which sooner or later becomes its equal or its superior. But kindness works simply and perseveringly; it produces no strained relations which prejudice its working; strained relations which already exist it relaxes. Mistrust and mis-understanding it puts to flight, and it strengthens itself by calling forth answering kindness, hence it is the furthest-reaching and most effective of all forces.

Today's passage anticipates the teaching of Jesus in the Sermon on the Mount, and Paul quotes directly from it in Romans 12:20. Can we find better, or harder, sentiments than these to put into practice?

The Tongue

....

'Without wood, a fire goes out; without gossip, quarrelling stops. . . .
Gossip is so tasty! How we love to swallow it!' (vv. 20, 22, GNB).

Olive Wyon writes in *On the Way*:

Nothing does more harm to our neighbour and to our own spiritual
life than the undisciplined use of the tongue. Sometimes, when
prayer becomes difficult or distasteful, on a little reflection we may
discover that this is due to some recent conversation in which we
have said something that is not quite true, or is exaggerated, or
even malicious or uncharitable.

Worshipping together is a delight and, for many, there is a chance to
catch up on the latest news about everyone: what your friends have
done, or failed to do. Animated discussion is part and parcel of the
Christian life. Without it we feel isolated, become introverted to an
unhealthy degree and lose some of the joy which belongs to those who
serve Jesus.

Let's always ensure that such talk is harmless, not simply gossip. As
we inquire after our neighbour, let's remember the prayer of Francis of
Assisi:

> Lord, make me an instrument of your peace,
> Where there is hatred let me sow love,
> Where there is injury, pardon;
> Where there is doubt, faith;
> Where there is despair, hope;
> Where there is darkness, light;
> Where there is sadness, joy.
> For it is in giving that we receive;
> It is in pardoning that we are pardoned;
> It is in dying that we are born to eternal life.

Feminism – Old Testament Style

'She considers a field and buys it; out of her earnings she plants a vineyard . . . Give her the reward she has earned, and let her works bring her praise at the city gate' (vv. 16, 31).

The domestic nature of this hymn praising the good wife may bring scathing rebuke from modern feminists, but see how the woman's influence extends. Not just the house, but also the vineyard and the market place, where she is entitled to the rewards she has earned.

Her husband, it is assumed, sits in judgment at the gate of the city – the equivalent of a modern law court – so there was a long way to go before women would have equality. Women were not expected to have power within the legal system – an area where the judgment of a good woman can make an enormous difference.

We must go beyond the ancient wisdom of Proverbs to fully appreciate the relationship with God and with others now open to us. We are dwarfs on giant's shoulders: we may not be as wise as the giants of the past who gave us the book of Proverbs, but because we stand on their shoulders we can see further than they did.

How necessary it is for women not only to be accorded a secure place within society – as envisaged in Proverbs – but for their skills and abilities to be used throughout society. Such thinking was pioneered in the nineteenth century by such women as Catherine Booth, co-founder of The Salvation Army, but much of today's world is still male-dominated.

However, even if full participation by women is still in the future we do well to ponder the final verse of Proverbs. Don't exploit her: 'Give her the reward she has earned.' Not just equal pay for equal work, but even more importantly, equal opportunity, in education, employment and power.

Think First

....

*'You are not a God who takes pleasure in evil . . . the arrogant
cannot stand in your presence' (vv. 4, 5).*

Sadly, we disappoint God sometimes. We don't mean to, we just can't
resist the temptation to demonstrate our cleverness, and someone
gets hurt. It's not Christlike. That's not something we learned from
Jesus. Sure, Jesus could speak sharply when the occasion merited it.
The traders in the temple felt the cutting edge of his tongue. But no
one who did not deserve criticism received it from him. No one was
made to feel small in order to make him look great. That's what we
should learn from him.

Too Sharp

I spoke too quickly
And my 'witty' words,
So sharp and shiny,
Hurt a friend of mine.
I didn't think
About his finer feelings
Or I'd have bitten off
My tongue in time!
My teasing sometimes
Runs away with me
And in its wake
Brings someone misery.

My friend forgives me
Freely, Lord, and yet
His disappointed eyes
I can't forget.

Judas and James

Introduction

We twenty-first century disciples have much to learn from those followers of Jesus who knew him well. The original twelve who accompanied Jesus on his teaching ministry throughout Galilee knew him best and observed him most closely.

Some of Christ's disciples we know better than others. Some are almost a closed book to us, since little is recorded of them. Judas is a man of mystery. Has he been misjudged down the centuries for his betrayal of Jesus? Is it simply that Satan entered into him and he became a lost soul? We ponder these thoughts.

James was one of our Lord's brothers but was not supportive of Jesus during his early ministry. John's Gospel makes the point that even his own brothers did not believe in Jesus (7:5). But that was to change. Among those disciples who were found with the apostles in Jerusalem following the Lord's ascension were Jesus' brothers (Acts 1:14). Later, James was to play a prominent role in the church at Jerusalem. He is worthy of study.

These readings are from the pen of Commissioner Harry Read and were first published in *Words of Life* in April 1999.

For the Sunday readings, John Gowans continues to provide a prayer-poem with a selected Bible passage.

The Last-Named

....

'And Judas Iscariot, who betrayed him' (v. 19).

Matthew, Mark and Luke all list the disciples (see also Matthew 10:2-4; Luke 6:14-16), and all three make Judas the last-named. Even though someone's name has to be last, it is assumed that Judas occupies that position because of his infamy. Each list identifies him as a traitor.

Judas is something of a mystery. It remains beyond our understanding that a man could spend so much time with Jesus and then betray him. How could he possibly be in the company of the most noble person the world has known, be the object of our Lord's prayers and still find it in his heart to betray him to the authorities?

In a sense, Judas was the odd man out in the disciple group in so far as he was the only non-Galilean Jesus called to apostleship. Iscariot means 'a man of Kerioth' and two places bear that name: one is located in the south of Judah and the other in the land of Moab. Being from a different area, however, was no excuse for betrayal.

Judas was called by Jesus in the same way as the other eleven were called. Luke observes that it was after Jesus had spent a night in prayer (Luke 6:12), and Mark states: 'He appointed twelve – designating them apostles – that they might be with him and that he might send them out to preach and to have authority to drive out demons' (Mark 3:14, 15). Clearly, Jesus saw in Judas qualities which, if rightly directed, would enable him to function adequately as an apostle.

Jesus probably saw a great deal more, as he does within all of us, but at the time of his call to apostleship Judas had equal footing with his peers. As with the others, he had the potential to be a saint.

....

There is within each of us
A vast potential to do good,
To live a life victorious,
God's love and mercy understood.
In love God wills our lives should be
Marked by his love's prosperity.

H. R.

Common Ground

....

'And Judas Iscariot, who became a traitor' (v. 16).

We do not know where Judas first met Jesus, but clearly there was such a meeting. Judas must have done something notable to catch our Lord's attention. Perhaps he had listened with an unusual concentration, asking a question here and there. Perhaps he discussed with the other disciples our Lord's teaching and mission.

We can only guess, but at the time Jesus drew up his shortlist for the disciple group Judas had done enough to warrant consideration, and our Lord's night of prayer (v. 12) confirmed that he was suitable for inclusion. Like the others, he had been drawn to Jesus, and Jesus was drawn to him.

When Judas' hopes were stirred, what, we wonder, did he envisage? It has been suggested that he saw Jesus as Israel's deliverer from Roman power, but if that was true he was not alone in the view. Cleopas and his companion, for instance, who left Jerusalem for Emmaus on Easter Day thought the same (Luke 24:21). Judas must surely have felt his spirit lifted in the presence of Jesus and been drawn by his other-worldliness.

....

O Judas, did you not have dreams
Of what the future had in store?
Fair dreams of influence and grace,
The best things from life's treasure store?

Did you not dream that all your peers
Would hold your name in high esteem
And after you their children name?
Is this not how evolved your dream?

Did you not dream that God himself
Would bless you for your well-earned fame,
Your wisdom and your faithfulness,
The rich associations of your name?

But noble dreams should help us choose
Right things to do; right words to say,
Not lead us down a shameful path
Where we the Son of God betray.

H. R.

Out of Step

....

'But one of his disciples, Judas Iscariot, who was later to betray him, objected, "Why wasn't this perfume sold and the money given to the poor? It was worth a year's wages"' (vv. 4, 5).

Such was our Lord's confidence in Judas that, instead of him being on the fringe of the disciple group, he was given the task of treasurer. Because of this important role Judas was brought into prominence and given a voice which otherwise he would not have had. There was, however, a touch of avarice in his soul. John put it more strongly, describing him as a thief because he took money from the common purse (v. 6).

Of this we can be sure: long before this occasion when Mary took a 'pint of pure nard . . . poured it on Jesus' feet and wiped his feet with her hair' (v. 3), Judas was separated in spirit from his Master. He lacked the insight or the will to read spiritual messages into events. Instead of being moved by the sight of our Lord's anointing by Mary, he could only criticise.

Had he simply discerned gratitude and adoration in Mary's action it would have been sufficient; instead, he was concerned with material things and missed the inner truth. In fact, the spiritual message was far deeper than gratitude and adoration. Jesus perceived it as the preliminary anointing for his burial (v. 7).

We do not know how badly Judas took the Master's kindly rebuke, but he would be aware of the gulf between himself and the Lord. Would he be aware, also, of the fact that Jesus, who knew what lay in the hearts of men (John 2:24, 25), was sadly aware of the thoughts crystallising in this disciple's mind (6:70, 71)?

How Christ must have laboured for Judas in prayer! He would not easily surrender to Satan one who had shown such promise, and whom he had previously regarded with so much confidence.

....

Sin casts a veil across the eyes
And crucial truths remain unseen,
It is the end, the sad demise
Of all the good that might have been.
Our hearts must be kept sensitive
If with the Christ we want to live.

H. R.

An Unyielding Heart

> 'After he had said this, Jesus was troubled in spirit and testified,
> "I tell you the truth, one of you is going to betray me"' (v. 21).

We marvel at the fact that, of all the pressing issues which could have troubled the mind and heart of Jesus in the Upper Room at that moment, he confessed to but one, and that was his imminent betrayal by Judas. Why could he not shut Judas out of his mind or convince himself that Judas had chosen to be a lost soul who, by his own choice, had made the ancient prophesy of his betrayal come true (v. 18; see Psalm 41:9)?

There were no doubt so many thoughts in his mind clamouring for expression before the moment of his capture, but surely the Christ was deeply troubled because it was a friend who was going to betray him.

It was not for himself that Jesus was troubled; he knew that to be crucified was to be glorified (vv. 31, 32). Even though he believed that his betrayal was inevitable and had declared 'Woe to that man who betrays the Son of Man! It would be better for him if he had not been born' (Mark 14:21), Jesus still felt for Judas. He could not shed his role as the Good Shepherd and lightly accept the fact that he was losing one of his sheep. He was deeply wounded and troubled in his spirit.

Is it too fanciful to imagine that in all the tense, dramatic moments which lay ahead of him, Jesus continued to be aware of Judas, and that the wound Judas had inflicted would be even more painful than those the soldiers were to inflict at his scourging? If ever we needed a reminder of the tender heart of Jesus, we have it here in his confession to his disciples that he was troubled in spirit because 'one of you is going to betray me' (v. 21).

No story illustrates the need for the Incarnation more than the story of Judas and his personal tragedy.

The wilful heart of man
Has always troubled Christ.
For this he came to earth,
For this was sacrificed.
There is no other remedy
To save man from sin's tragedy.

H. R.

An Interesting Theory

'As soon as Judas took the bread, Satan entered into him. "What you are about to do, do quickly," Jesus told him' (John 13:27).

There have been those who have considered Judas to be a good, albeit misguided man, and they have endeavoured to interpret his actions in that light. One theory portrays Judas as a man who believed Jesus to be the Messiah, the King born of the line of David who would lead the rebellion against Rome and be crowned King of Israel. Judas, so the theory runs, began to feel that Jesus was slow to capitalise on the support he was receiving, and that the time was ripe for him to take steps to commence the rebellion, especially after the public display of emotion and expectation on Palm Sunday (John 12:12, 13).

Greatly concerned that Jesus was missing his moment of destiny, Judas decided to take things into his own hands and create the circumstances that would make it necessary for Jesus to declare himself. For this reason, so the theory continues, Judas decided to betray Jesus and, once in his enemies' hands, Jesus would have to declare himself, take control of the situation, allow the people to make him King, commence the rebellion, and all would be well thereafter. However, this attempt to portray Judas in such favourable terms has no support in Scripture.

The biblical record supports John's contention that after Judas had received the morsel of bread which Jesus handed to him in fellowship, Satan entered into him and he became a lost soul. Matthew's account of Judas seeking out the chief priests to make a deal with them (Matthew 26:14–16) leaves little room for generous thought. Judas perversely chose to betray his Master, and his remorse when Jesus was condemned (27:3, 4) remains the only redeeming fact Scripture records of him.

We do not know poor Judas's motivation.
The kind of energy that drove his soul,
Be it plain evil or false aspiration,
We only know he filled the traitor's role.
Nor dare we judge him for the road he trod,
But leave him to the mercy of our God.

H. R.

A Friend's Greeting

*'Now the betrayer had arranged a signal with them: "The one
I kiss is the man; arrest him." Going at once to Jesus, Judas said,
"Greetings, Rabbi!" and kissed him' (vv. 48, 49).*

It has been pointed out that Judas always addressed Jesus as Rabbi, a
name which means teacher. Others called him Lord; not so Judas
(see v. 25). Perhaps that is a significant factor in his behaviour: he
failed to recognise the Christ in his eternal role. We also wonder why,
when the time for betrayal arrived, he chose to identify Jesus with a
kiss.

Judas could have so easily remained in the background, because
even at night-time Jesus would be a distinctive enough figure for him
to point out to the soldiers. Another alternative would have been for
the soldiers to surround the Lord's group and ask Jesus to identify
himself, which of course he would have done.

What strange, perverse reason caused him to kiss Jesus unless John's
words were completely true: 'Satan entered into him' (John 13:27)?
The forces of darkness must have rejoiced at that moment.

We note our Lord's restraint when he received the kiss. We would
have reacted with horror and distaste, turning away from contact,
except perhaps to push him away. Our minds would have been seeking
a caustic comment to put this hateful man in the worst possible light,
but Jesus, in full control of the situation, simply said, 'Friend, do what
you came for' (Matthew 26:50).

He accepted Judas in his role of betrayer knowing that a prophecy
was being fulfilled (v. 54), although his heart must have been heavy
because it had come to pass (John 13:18–22). That prophecy, and how
anyone could be destined to betray the Messiah, is something of a
mystery but I am confident that neither Judas nor anyone else was
born to that shameful task. God is not like that, but he knows that
Judas-like people, though rare, exist in every generation.

'Surely not I, Lord?' each disciple asked
When Jesus said one would his Lord betray.
Had not each in the Master's glory basked
And shared the Master's mission every day?
But if allegiance can divided be,
There is no limit to disloyalty.

H. R.

Right But Wrong

....

*'O LORD, do not rebuke me in your anger . . . be merciful to me . . .
   deliver me; save me because of your unfailing love' (vv. 1, 2, 4).*

If only we were as eager to demonstrate love to our neighbour as we
are to receive it from our God. We want to be shown mercy but
sometimes fail to display it to others. Jesus told us our daily prayer
should be: 'Forgive us the wrong we have done, as we have forgiven
those who have wronged us' (Matthew 6:12, *NEB*). But sometimes we
demand our rights while forgetting our responsibilities. When we
receive without giving, when we 'win' by bulldozer tactics, we should
not be surprised if the 'victory' has a hollow feel about it.

Victory

I got my way!
They finally gave in
And I have won!
But strange to say
I don't feel all that pleased
With what I've done.
I raised my voice,
Made my position clear,
And I was right, of course,
And wrong, I fear!

My case was just,
But my bulldozer way
Of getting what I want
Was wrong, you say?

And is that why
My vict'ry can't be sung,
And its sweet taste
Is sawdust on my tongue?

Worlds Apart

....

'Then Satan entered Judas, called Iscariot' (v. 3).

The story of Judas is the story of two worlds – the world of a fallen humanity and the world of a redeeming love. Because we are related to both worlds, Judas is representative of the best and worst within us. The noblest, most sensitive elements within Judas were drawn to Christ. There is no record of when or where he first came into contact with the Master but, like the others, he must have been impressed by our Lord's other-worldliness. His aspirations were stimulated and he was captivated by the simplicity, integrity and godliness Jesus exuded.

It is possible that Judas was among the number who have difficulty in committing themselves totally to an ideal, a cause or a person. Whatever his problem was, however, he fell prey to his lower nature and, if he thought he could take Jesus on his own terms, he was to find that the Lord's values were not negotiable. Perhaps it was a mixture of greed, resentment and satanic domination (v. 3; John 13:2) which led him to betrayal.

The contrast between good and evil is most clearly defined by Jesus in his attitude towards Judas. Our Lord has never been slow to call to him those who find faith difficult (see John 20:26, 27), and he worked hard to produce love and faith in them.

It will be recalled that when Jesus met with the disciples in the Upper Room and the men were reluctant to wash each other's feet, it was he who fulfilled this simple task, kneeling before each man in turn – including Judas. As the semi-private dialogue recorded by John seems to indicate (John 13:22–29), Jesus even gave Judas an honoured place beside him at the table. Although he knew that Judas was going to betray him, Jesus never failed to show a tender, infinite love towards him. Even so, Judas proved himself capable of ignoring that love.

....

I would, Lord, serve you well,
For love of you, not love of gain,
I would your love and mercy tell,
Betray you not and cause you pain.
For you are hope and life to me,
My peace, my joy, my destiny.

H. R.

An Important Reminder

*'Concerning Judas, who served as guide for those who arrested Jesus –
he was one of our number and shared in this ministry' (vv. 16, 17).*

There was no doubt in Peter's mind that Judas, in spite of his villainy
(v. 18, *NEB*), had been a genuine member of the disciple group. If
ever Judas felt isolated because he was not a Galilean, the others
seemed not to be aware of it. Not only was Judas 'one of our number'
but 'he shared in this ministry'.

When Jesus sent the disciples out in twos (Matthew 10:4), Simon the
Zealot and Judas probably went together. We can be sure that the
pairing of the disciples was carefully made so that the disciples felt
comfortable with each other and complemented each other's ministry.
There is no evidence to suggest that Simon and Judas exercised a
substandard ministry. Judas was a full member of the group in every
respect.

In the prayer made before the drawing of lots to identify Judas'
successor, reference was made to the fact that he *abandoned* his
ministry and apostleship (1:25, *NEB*). Clearly it was believed that,
although a prophecy was being fulfilled (v. 16), Judas was not in the
grip of forces over which he had no control but had exercised a
personal choice. He betrayed Christ of his own volition. The
responsibility was his alone.

The freedom of choice with which God honours us has enormous
consequences. The prayer made before the lots were drawn concluded
with 'which Judas left to go *where he belongs*' (v. 25). Personal choice
determines destiny. We can choose to be numbered among the Lord's
people and share his ministry, or we can choose to disregard or
abandon the call he has given to us. How good it is that we have the
Holy Spirit striving within us to help us make the right choice! Even
so, the choice is ours.

> Am I not free to choose,
> To Christ our Saviour cleave
> Or that same Saviour leave
> And all his blessing lose?
> Lord, let my choice for ever be
> To follow you obediently.
>
> *H. R.*

The Replacement for Judas

'Peter stood up among the believers . . . and said, "Brothers, the Scripture had to be fulfilled"' (vv. 15, 16).

Judas had died, either by his own hand (Matthew 27:5) or in a mysterious and awful way (Acts 1:18) or, as some scholars suggest, by a combination of the two accounts. In Peter's judgment the time had come for Judas to be replaced in the apostolic group.

We pause to consider the scene. They met in the Upper Room where some of them had been staying (v. 13), that is, lodging (*NEB*). The disciple group was augmented by our Lord's mother, Mary, and the other women who had been so loyal to him. Included also were the brothers of Jesus (vv. 13, 14). Luke, the historian, defines the 'believers' who gathered as a group of some one hundred and twenty people (v. 15).

Because the conditions Peter laid down for apostleship related to those men who 'have been with us the whole time the Lord Jesus went in and out among us, beginning from John's baptism to the time when Jesus was taken up from us' (vv. 21, 22), we begin to understand that, as Jesus moved around the country, a large group of devoted men and women was in constant attendance, in addition to the disciples.

We could speculate at length concerning this group of worthy people, many of whom Jesus would consider for apostleship before finally selecting the twelve. They had no formal recognition, but their presence would be an encouragement to the Master. They were loyal people, intent on learning the Lord's ways.

Presumably, they were caught up in the tragedy of the crucifixion and the triumph of the resurrection and were welcomed into the close fellowship of prayer and expectation concerning the outpouring of the Spirit. It was to this extended and devoted group that Peter spoke about the replacement for Judas.

More follow Christ than we imagine,
More than we think before him bow;
The Upper Room stands as a token
Of nameless hands upon his plough.
Our anonymity no slur implies
We all are very precious in his eyes.

H. R.

Matthias

. . . .

'Therefore it is necessary to choose one of the men who have been with us the whole time the Lord Jesus went in and out among us' (v. 21).

As with many scriptural accounts, we wish the writer had given more information. A modern writer would have dwelt on the atmosphere, described the selection processes and given us a resume of each candidate's qualifications. Not so the Scriptures – the historians had their eyes on larger issues and wrote sparingly. Even so, we would have liked a fuller account.

Clearly, there was little to choose between Justus and Matthias, the two men whom the company considered to be worthy of apostleship. Both had been with Jesus from the beginning – perhaps they had been disciples of John the Baptist also, perhaps not – but they were among the men from whom Jesus had chosen his original twelve and, in spite of being passed over for that privilege, had continued with him (see John 6:66). They were witnesses to his miracles, beneficiaries of his teaching, had witnessed his death, resurrection and ascension and, in consequence, were well qualified for apostleship (v. 22).

We do not know precisely what Luke meant by casting lots. It is possible that after prayer had been made the two names, Matthias and Justus, were placed in a container and the company was willing to believe that whichever name was uppermost when the lots were cast, God had made that person his choice.

Within a short time the Holy Spirit came to guide his people and the system of casting lots was discontinued, but Matthias would be accepted as a properly chosen apostle. It matters not that we do not read of him again; some other disciples are not mentioned either, but each man had his own role to fill.

. . . .

How blessed we are to have
The Holy Spirit as our guide,
Who gives us wisdom from above
And helps us rightly to decide.
Our choices can be made with confidence
Because the Spirit wields his influence.

H. R.

James – the Lord's Brother

'Then he appeared to James' (v. 7).

In the Gospels our awareness of the family of Jesus is due almost entirely to the fact that, sadly, they did not believe in him. Both Matthew (13:55) and Mark (6:3) name the brothers – James, Joseph, Simon and Judas – and refer to his sisters (whom they failed to name) in connection with our Lord's return to Nazareth, his home town. Although the Nazarenes were enormously impressed by his teaching they could not accept him because they knew him as the carpenter's son and knew his family.

The Lord's brothers encouraged Jesus to go to Jerusalem at a time which would not have been right for him and, when recording the incident, John made the clear statement, 'even his own brothers did not believe in him' (John 7:5).

We can be sure that just as Mary, the Lord's mother, kept in touch with him, the family did also. It is possible that they were included in the group which witnessed the crucifixion (Luke 23:49) and, most certainly, the brothers were in the Upper Room as part of the praying company (Acts 1:14) after our Lord's ascension, and before the Spirit descended at Pentecost.

It is of considerable interest and importance that, among the many to whom Jesus appeared after his resurrection, James, his younger brother, should be one of them. We can understand the Lord's concern that his own family should be numbered among the redeemed, and a resurrection appearance to James would be enough to bring his doubting family into the fold.

We also read into this event the lovely truth that of our Lord's personal appearances one was to Peter who had denied him, another was to James who had disbelieved him, and yet another was to Saul who had opposed him. The Good Shepherd's love is so vast and tender!

> You have time, Lord,
> Time for those who failed to be their best,
> Who failed faith's strong and searching test;
> Time for those who disregarded you,
> Opposing all you tried to do.
> You have both time and love, Lord.
>
> H. R.

James – his Importance

*'Someone told him, "Your mother and brothers are
standing outside, wanting to speak to you"' (v. 47).*

Our Lord's reaction to the message that his mother and brothers
wanted to speak with him was to turn to the disciples and say,
'Here are my mother and my brothers. For whoever does the will of
my Father in heaven is my brother and sister and mother' (vv. 49,
50). At that time our Lord's family was out of harmony with his mission and
he had a point to make, but he was tender towards his family. This
concern is illustrated by the way in which he took time, while being
crucified, to commit his mother into the care of his disciple John (John
19:25–27), and by his post-resurrection appearance to his brother
James (1 Corinthians 15:7).

Reasons advanced by scholars concerning our Lord's commitment of
Mary to John instead of to her son, James, differ. One reason hinges
on the fact that the brothers were at variance with Jesus at the time,
but Jesus appeared to James shortly afterwards to rectify that. Of
greater importance, perhaps, was our Lord's knowledge that John was
to live to a great age, whereas James would be martyred in the not-too-
distant future. Whatever the true reason, we can be assured that Mary,
James and John would know our Lord's action was for the best.

James's discipleship – indeed, apostleship (see Galatians 1:17–19) –
was important to Jesus and the early Church. If it could have been
asserted that even Christ's family, those who knew him best, could not
be persuaded that his claims were true, it would be a damaging
argument against the gospel. If, on the other hand, there was a strong
witness from the family, that he whom they had known so well in the
close confines of the home was, in their considered judgment, the Son
of God and Saviour of the world, the Church had additional grounds for
confidence.

If within a family
The life of Christ is seen,
Spotless in its purity,
With nothing harsh or mean,
We can be sure that in such care
The Spirit of the Lord is there.
H. R.

Second Chance

....

'If you, O Lord, kept a record of sins, O Lord, who could stand?
But with you there is forgiveness' (vv. 3, 4).

In our natural state we humans are pretty unforgiving. A few people put the rest to shame by their gracious, forgiving nature, but most of us find it hard to forgive and forget. There's no excuse for this – the example given to us by our Creator couldn't be clearer, and the life of Jesus dispels any doubt about divine nature. Christianity has been called the Gospel of the Second Chance. We should demonstrate it in our dealings with others, as well as take advantage of it for ourselves.

Trust

It's very sad
But it was my mistake.
I trusted someone
And he let me fall.
I've got my bruises
But I'm wiser now.
I'll not trust him again,
Not him! That's all.

But this won't do
For, Lord, how would it be
If you applied
The silly rule to me?

James – Church Leader

'Peter motioned with his hand for them to be quiet . . . "Tell James and the brothers about this," he said' (v. 17).

Members of the immediate family of Jesus would have a special status within the ever-growing band of believers. Their reluctance to identify with Jesus during his lifetime would be well known, but their subsequent conversion and allegiance would be seen as a powerful endorsement of Christ's claims.

Even so, unless they were exceptionally gifted, they would not be granted leadership roles. We note, for instance, that the other three brothers, Joseph and Simon and Judas (Matthew 13:55), were afforded no high-profile tasks, although Judas wrote the small Epistle that bears his name. James, however, from the beginning, was a man of outstanding ability and influence.

Although Peter's leadership in the disciple group and in the earliest days of the Church was obvious and acceptable (Acts 1:15; 2:14; 3:1-7; 4:8; 5:3), soon he was sharing the leadership position with James, and doing so without difficulty. Obviously, James was a leader, large of spirit and of great wisdom. It could not have been much later than AD 36-37 when Paul, having been converted three years earlier, made his way to Jerusalem to meet Peter. He stayed with Peter for fifteen days, and subsequently stated that he saw none of the other apostles except 'James, the Lord's brother' (Galatians 1:19). Later in his letter to the Galatians, Paul seems to be indicating that James was the acknowledged leader of the church in Jerusalem (2:12).

At the Council of Jerusalem (Acts 15:1ff.), where the Gentile problems with Jewish customs were resolved, the record makes it abundantly clear that James was the leader of the Jerusalem church. Our Lord's opposing brother had come a long way!

Once out of step, now in accord,
The brother called his brother, Lord;
He prayed to him for added grace,
Maintained his Lord's exalted place
And for the man whose family name he bore,
James lived and died – and lives for evermore.

H. R.

James – the Listener

••

'When they finished, James spoke up: "Brothers, listen to me"' (v. 13).

The Council of Jerusalem was one of the crucial events in the development of the new Church. Inadequate listening leading to a wrong decision could have arrested the growth of the new community and the major burden of decision-making rested with James. By this time he was the recognised head of the church in Jerusalem (vv. 13, 19); some have actually described him as the first Bishop of Jerusalem. If ever James needed statesmanlike qualities, he needed them at this council.

It will be recalled that the crisis had arisen because Jewish Christians visited the Gentile Christians in Antioch and said: 'Unless you are circumcised, according to the custom taught by Moses, you cannot be saved' (v. 1). This statement was so contrary to the gospel that Paul, Barnabas and Peter contested it keenly, both in and out of the council (vv. 2–12).

There is an art in listening and it appears as though James had mastered it. He needed no reminder that this was a vital issue which had to be handled with integrity, discernment and tact. We visualise him, therefore, listening intently with his head and heart, giving full value to the testimony of the legalists and those who emphasised the freedom of the gospel. With the good listener's skill, he would be evaluating the atmosphere of the assembly as they too listened intently (v. 12), and he would be reaching out to the Holy Spirit for guidance.

That James had listened well is shown by his measured response: 'Brothers, listen to me' (v. 13). Although opposing views had been expressed, they were brothers in Christ and belonged to each other still. They were ready to receive James's decision.

••

> There is a way of listening
> Whereby each salient point is heard,
> And wisdom comes refreshingly
> To add new insights to each word.
> Such listening is a consecrated art –
> Of good decisions a most vital part.
>
> *H. R.*

James – Decision-Maker

....

'It is my judgment, therefore, that we should not make it difficult for the Gentiles who are turning to God' (v. 19).

Although James intended to make a decision in favour of the gospel's freedom rather than adherence to the Jewish law, James handled the legalists so that they would not feel as though they were being dismissed. Wisely, James made reference to the report made by Peter. If any in the assembly were contrasting Peter's previous high status as the church leader with his current position as subordinate to James, their feelings would be largely mollified by James's acknowledgement of the prime contribution Peter had made to the council (v. 14).

In his summing-up, James quoted verses from the prophet Amos which confirmed God's plans for the Gentiles (vv. 16–18). The legalists would not quarrel with Amos! In addition, James made the reasonable statement that 'we should not make it difficult for the Gentiles who are turning to God' (v. 19). Jewish Christians would agree with that, and Gentiles would be delighted with it. James then laid down three conditions for the Gentiles to accept. They were to abstain from food polluted by idols, from sexual immorality, and meat of strangled animals and blood (v. 20). The legalists would see that as a fair compromise, and the Gentiles would probably think that the first two conditions were sound, and the last of insufficient importance to resist.

The wisdom of James's decision and the thoughtful way in which it was presented led to its trouble-free implementation. When the Christians of Antioch received James's letter giving his decision they 'were glad for its encouraging message' (v. 31). Judas and Silas proved to be ideal couriers in so far as they moved around encouraging the people and, when they returned to Jerusalem, they did so with a blessing of peace (vv. 33, 34).

....

When problems are resolved
With wisdom and with care,
When our blest Guide becomes involved
And we make earnest prayer,
Decisions made are for the best
And, usually, they stand time's test.

H. R.

James – the Martyr

*'After spending some time there, they were sent off by the
brothers with the blessing of peace to return to those
who had sent them' (v. 33).*

The 'blessing of peace' would be much valued by Judas and Silas as
they returned home because life there was becoming very tense. So
tense that for the Christians in Jerusalem the martyrdom of Stephen
and the earlier persecution (7:1ff.; 8:1–4) would occupy their thoughts;
as would the death of James, the brother of John (12:2), who was the
first apostle to be martyred.

As the Christian Church won more converts from Judaism (21:20),
Judaism became increasingly resistant to the gospel, and the threat of
conflict intensified. James, the Lord's brother, as the head of the
Church would be conscious of the frailty of Jerusalem's peace. At any
time, either the civil or Jewish authorities could move against him and
those under his care. There is a tradition which says that James was a
great intercessor, spending so much time on his knees praying for his
people that his knees became misshapen. Clearly, such prayer was
needed.

According to tradition it was not the civil rulers who moved against
James, but, defying the law (see John 18:31), the Scribes and Pharisees
took action. When Jesus was tempted he was led by Satan to the
pinnacle of the temple where he was invited to cast himself down so
that angels might rescue him (Luke 4:9–11). Not so James, the Lord's
brother; he was taken to the pinnacle of the temple and thrown down.
So died a man of great faith.

One of the powerful arguments in support of Christ's claims to be
Lord and Saviour is that those who knew him best were willing to die
for him. So sure were Stephen, James the brother of John, James the
Lord's brother, Peter, Andrew and then Paul that Jesus was Lord, that
the threat of death left them undismayed. To deny his Lordship was to
lose everything.

As those brave men were sure that you were Lord,
So make me sure that you are Lord and Christ.
And let your life in me be my reward,
My right to rule myself be sacrificed.

H. R.

A Pause for Reflection

'James, Peter and John, those reputed to be pillars, gave me and Barnabas the right hand of fellowship' (v. 9).

Our key verse shows clearly that James, formerly a disbeliever and critic, had taken precedence over Peter and John in the leadership of the Church. As we reflect on James's life, three important truths present themselves for our consideration.

The first truth is that it is possible to know much about Jesus and still not call him Lord. James had been exposed to the quality of his brother's life and, though others believed in him, he did not. There have been, and no doubt are, many people who know of Jesus, respect him for his goodness, influence and spirituality, but still do not call him Lord.

Second, in spite of James's disbelief, Jesus wanted to win him to his side, hence the special appearance after the resurrection (1 Corinthians 15:7). From personal experience we know how thoughtfully Jesus works to reveal himself in his risen glory. Not quite as he visited James, but as he chose to come to us.

The third truth we consider is that when we acknowledge him as Lord, the vast potential of our lives moves towards fulfilment; our capacities are enlarged and the 'greater things' of which Jesus spoke (John 14:12) become possible to us.

Who could have seen in James, the unbeliever (John 7:5), the man who one day would become the leader of the Church in Jerusalem, masterminding its opportunity and handling its problems? When Christ has our all he is able to make his all available to us.

He pushes out the boundaries of our minds,
Equips us with his gifts and his own love,
Removes the inward cataract that blinds
Our sight to all that we can be and daily prove.
Who knows the Lord, life's secret truly finds.

H. R.

When God was Seen on Earth

Introduction

'Christmas comes but once a year' is a phrase known to millions of people, though probably few could identify its source as the title of a poem by nineteenth-century poet Elizabeth R. Parkes (real name Bessie Rayner Belloc). It's quite a political poem that contrasts the Christmas celebrations of rich and poor people, and urges the wealthy to remember the 'have nots'. I rather think the Christ himself would approve of the sentiments! Reading the poem might put you in the right frame of mind to ponder the thoughts expressed on the pages that follow.

Advent is a good time to remember that Christmas is not such a straightforward, simplistic season as some would have us believe. There is much mystery to which we might address our minds, and Mary particularly is worthy of a deeper scrutiny than many Protestant Christians have subjected her to.

As this season comes but once a year, let's use these days wisely while we recall when God was seen on earth.

> When God was seen in Bethlehem,
> He came a perfect stranger,
> He wrapped himself in swaddling clothes
> And laid him in a manger.
>
> Whatever did they say to him?
> Did they kneel down and pray to him
> Upon the cattle's hay, to him
> When God was seen on earth?
>
> They had not quite expected him,
> They just kind of neglected him,
> You might say they rejected him
> When God was seen on earth.

In the Beginning

'In the beginning was the Word, and the Word was with God, and the Word was God. He was with God in the beginning . . . In him was life, and that life was the light of men . . . The true light that gives light to every man was coming into the world' (vv. 1, 2, 4, 9).

Today as we begin our Advent readings, it's important to start right at the very beginning. And that means not Bethlehem, where Jesus was born, or Nazareth, where the angel appeared to Mary and gave her the news that she was to be the earthly mother of the Messiah, but the very beginning of everything: even before the creation of the world, if we can imagine such a time.

Says the writer of John's Gospel: 'In the beginning was the Word, and the Word was with God, and the Word was God.'

The Word was Jesus, who John goes on to describe as 'the light of men'. And so we begin our Christmas readings with two metaphors: word and light. Both are helpful, both are mysterious. A one-time Bible teacher at The Salvation Army's officer training college in London was accustomed, when tackling a difficult question, to say: 'The answer is shrouded in mystery.' And so, indeed, it often is. Sir Winston Churchill once described Russia as 'a riddle wrapped in a mystery inside an enigma'. I confess some of the things of God seem equally impenetrable to the human mind. I imagine that is one of the reasons God came to earth as he did. As George MacDonald wrote, in a three-verse poem that has become a popular Christmas carol:

> They all were looking for a king
> To slay their foes and lift them high;
> Thou cam'st a little baby thing
> That made a woman cry.

Emmanuel – one of the names by which Jesus is called – means 'God with us'. How better could God have demonstrated the truth that he was – is – incarnate among us than by coming as a human child? As we approach Christmas let's rejoice in the glorious reality at its heart: 'God with us'.

Choice

....

*'If I settle on the far side of the sea, even there your hand will guide
me, your right hand will hold me fast' (vv. 9, 10).*

One of the paradoxes of our faith is that God stands ready to provide
all the help we need to live successful, fulfilled and meaningful
lives – and wants nothing more than to do so – but he will not force his
aid upon us. As Psalm 139 declares, his hand will guide us and hold us
fast; but five millennia of history reveals that if men and women
choose to go their own, errant, way, he will not intervene. He loves us
too much to take back his gift of free will.

Instinct

No one need tell the sunflower
What is dark and what is bright.
Instinctively he knows and turns
His face towards the light.

And no one marks the map to tell
The swallow where to go.
Instinctively she senses things,
She simply seems to know!

It's really much the same with me,
I know what's wrong, what's right.
The diff'rence is that I can choose
To turn against the light.

Jesus Foretold

••

*'God sent the angel Gabriel to Nazareth, a town in Galilee, to a
virgin pledged to be married to a man named Joseph, a descendant of
David. The virgin's name was Mary. The angel went to her and
said, "Greetings, you who are highly favoured! The Lord is with you"'
(vv. 26–28).*

Highly favoured! I wonder if that was how Mary felt at that moment
– this young virgin to whom an angel appears and turns her life
upside down with a story so incredible she could never even have
dreamed it. Mary must have asked herself: 'If this is a blessing, a
reward, what would a punishment be like?'

The angel tells her: 'The Holy Spirit will come upon you, and the
power of the Most High will overshadow you. So the holy one to be
born will be called the Son of God' (v. 35). It must be a hallucination.
A nightmare rather than a dream. Or else some kind of divine joke. A
cruel one. She is little more than a child. But she is to become a
mother, the mother of God's Son, no less. And not at some later stage
in her adult life when, just perhaps, she might be better able to cope.
No, the process has already begun. She will soon feel the divine child
moving within her.

How deep did her thoughts go? How well did she understand the
almost unsearchable truth that the God who created everything
needed – for reasons beyond Mary's comprehension, and perhaps ours
– a surrogate mother to enable him, through his Son, to experience the
reality of humanity? Was it blind faith, childlike faith, that motivated
her to say yes to the biggest request ever made of a human being? If
so, we should learn from it. God sometimes asks the greatest things of
the most ordinary people. Mary was no scholar, no theologian – but she
was a perfect mother, which was what God needed her to be.

Whatever I am, whatever God calls me to, I need to be that, for God's
sake, and the sake of the world he created.

••

To ponder:
**William Blake declared: 'Use what talents you possess. The
woods would be very silent if no birds sang there except those
that sang best.'**

Songs of Praise for Christmas

'And Mary said: "My soul glorifies the Lord and my spirit rejoices in God my Saviour, for he has been mindful of the humble state of his servant"' (vv. 46, 47).

A song or psalm or prayer was often written to mark important events both in the Old Testament and the New. The first ten verses of 1 Samuel 2 give us the song written for the dedication to God of Hannah's child, Samuel. It declares: 'There is no-one holy like the LORD; there is no-one besides you; there is no Rock like our God' (v. 2). And the song/prophecy composed by Zechariah for the birth of John the Baptist is recorded in Luke 1:67–79. It proclaims: 'And you, my child, will be called a prophet of the Most High; for you will go on before the Lord to prepare the way for him' (v. 76).

Mary's song is particularly beautiful. In it there is much of humility and mercy. Verses 52 and 53 tell us: 'He has brought down rulers from their thrones but has lifted up the humble. He has filled the hungry with good things but has sent the rich away empty.' Little wonder, perhaps, that during the 1980s the dictators of Guatemala outlawed its public reading because of its revolutionary tones. In Nicaragua, it is a favourite prayer among many peasants and is often carried as an amulet.

Known as the 'Magnificat' because that is the first word in the Latin version, Mary's song forms part of the daily office in the Roman Catholic vespers service and the Anglican service of evening prayer, and has been a popular text for many composers. Millions have had, and continue to have, cause to be grateful to Mary for sharing her thoughts in such a beautiful way.

Mary was grateful to God for the way he was 'mindful of the humble state of his servant'. He is no less mindful today, and we should be no less grateful.

He comes, the broken heart to bind,
The wounded soul to cure,
And with the treasures of his grace,
To enrich the humble poor.
Philip Doddridge

A Man to Admire

'An angel of the Lord appeared to him in a dream and said, "Joseph son of David, do not be afraid to take Mary home as your wife, because what is conceived in her is from the Holy Spirit"' (v. 20).

Mary was carefully chosen to be the mother of Jesus. And surely Joseph was just as meticulously selected to be the earthly father in what we call 'the holy family'. We can only imagine the initial shock that must have been his reaction when he learned that his pledged partner, in all her youthful innocence and purity, was 'with child'. No, let's use the clinical, honest word: his fiancée was pregnant, and he knew there was no chance that he was the father. Was he a fool? His family and friends would surely see it that way. We are told: 'Because Joseph her husband was a righteous man and did not want to expose her to public disgrace, he had in mind to divorce her quietly' (v. 19). If Joseph felt betrayed he had no intention of taking any sort of revenge. His love for Mary was as genuine as the tears he surely shed as he reached that decision.

When we talk of Joseph as a righteous man we should have in mind the Jewish meaning of that word as 'zealous' and 'quick to keep the rules'. However, in the case of Joseph, that righteousness was tempered by mercy. The rules allowed public judgment and death by stoning. But the angel of the Lord carefully explained to Joseph that Mary had not sinned – far from it – and Joseph should welcome her into his life. The son she carried was the child of God.

What an admirable man Joseph was! His acceptance of his destiny is followed by strange happenings at the child's birth, and then a dangerous flight into the foreign country of Egypt before an eventual return to his homeland and home town of Nazareth. A dozen quiet years will follow until he takes the child to the temple in Jerusalem, where more strange events will take place. And then will come years during which he will teach his 'son' – God's Son – his carpentry skills. Then Joseph will disappear from the written record. We assume he died before Jesus began his ministry. But 2,000 years later we are still thinking about Joseph, marvelling at him, and being inspired by him. He preached no sermon, wrote no Epistle, but left an eternal legacy of obedience and trust.

Silver Lining

'As there was no place for them inside the inn, she wrapped him up and laid him in a manger' (v. 7, JBP).

Not all the world belonged to the Roman Empire at that time, but a good part of it did, and their system of census was awesome. Caesar Augustus seemed to want to know exactly where every citizen and his wife lived – and not just Roman citizens, but all the occupants of conquered lands as well. And for some reason they had to be counted not where they were, but in the place they originally came from. Thus it was that Joseph had to travel from Nazareth to Bethlehem, taking his heavily pregnant wife with him. No one was excused such a journey.

The roads must have been chaotic, and it's little wonder the inns were overflowing. No one could book in advance in days before postal workers, let alone telephones and emails! To say Joseph must have been stressed would be an understatement. As well as the tiring journey, on foot, he had to close his carpentry business temporarily, losing valuable income. As it happened, the business was closed far longer than he expected, because of their emergency flight to Egypt to escape the wrath of a paranoid king. But that lay in the future the night Jesus was born.

The only silver lining that night was in the fact that a kind innkeeper gave them the shelter of his stable for their baby's birth. The presence of the animals did nothing for the hygiene of the place but at least produced some warmth! I guess Joseph and Mary were grateful for that.

Many things are relative, including wealth, health and comfort. Joseph and Mary's newborn baby was perfect: that was all that mattered to them. Just how perfect, of course, they had yet to discover. This Christmas, many people poor in the eyes of the world will count themselves rich as they celebrate with their families, while many 'rich' people will bemoan the fact that they are not rich enough. They never will be.

To pray:
'O come to my heart, Lord Jesus, there is room in my heart for thee.'

Emily Elizabeth Steele Elliott

The Watchers

....

'And there were shepherds living out in the fields near by,
keeping watch over their flocks at night. An angel of the Lord
appeared to them, and the glory of the Lord shone around them,
and they were terrified' (vv. 8, 9).

Shepherds were essential in first-century Palestine, but they were not always appreciated. Their employment prevented them keeping all the requirements of the Jewish faith with regard to things like attendance in the temple, observance of ceremonies and ritual cleanliness. They were often seen as little more than vagabonds.

They did one thing well. They were expert watchers. They looked out for wandering sheep, and watched that none was stolen. And they kept an eye out for wolves. They protected their sheep. They had to. That was their job, their livelihood. And although they did not observe all the religious rules, they were probably religious folk. People who stay out all night in dangerous circumstances usually are. Every soldier is a believer on the battlefield, so it is said.

Well, on the night the Messiah was born, the shepherds got their reward for all that watching. While the world slept, they saw angels. More importantly, they heard the angels' song and the angel's message: 'Do not be afraid. I bring you good news of great joy that will be for all the people. Today in the town of David a Saviour has been born to you; he is Christ the Lord' (vv. 10, 11).

And there we have it: it's good news for all the people, including those who slept through it. I'm glad the shepherds – the most ordinary of people – were the first to know. I take heart from that. It reinforces my belief that I'm important to God, and part of his plan. In a celebrity-driven world, it's good to know God doesn't have A-list and B-list people. His good news and his blessings are for all the people.

The biblical record of that event suggests there were more angels than shepherds present that night. Sometimes God announces his good news to just a few people at a time. Remember that this Christmas if you sing your carols in a tiny chapel rather than a great cathedral. Wherever you are, God is there – and probably some angels too, whether you recognise them or not.

Shepherds First

'The shepherds said to one another, "Let's go to Bethlehem and see this thing that has happened, which the Lord has told us about."
So they hurried off and found Mary and Joseph, and the baby, who was lying in the manger' (vv. 15, 16).

Who better than shepherds to find their way by night through the fields to a stable? They knew the paths, and they weren't afraid of the dark. They couldn't be in their job. But angels, now that was something new to them! We're all scared by things beyond our ken. But the shepherds had no doubt the angels – whoever they were – were real. And when they were told a special baby had been born and they would find him 'wrapped in cloths and lying in a manger' they believed what they were told. And they did as they were told!

And so it was that they were the first to pay homage to the Christ-child. For he was real too. The rich and the well-cultured and the wise would have their turn, but the shepherds – ordinary, humble, in fact slightly disreputable people – were first in line to see him and worship him. Later, that baby – when a man – would declare: 'The first shall be last, and the last shall be first.' The pattern was set at his birth.

Whatever the general public thought of shepherds – and shepherding in first-century Palestine wasn't the gentle, somewhat romantic occupation it is now seen as – Jesus had a lot of time for them. Later (see John 10:1–18) he described himself as 'the good shepherd; I know my sheep and my sheep know me . . . I lay down my life for the sheep.'

And so at Christmastime we find ourselves thinking ahead to Easter. So be it.

Let the foe not prevail, Shepherd, hear my prayer!
My resources would fail, Shepherd, hear my prayer!
Order all my steps aright,
Carry me from height to height;
Yonder shines the light!
Shepherd, lead me there! Lead me safely there!
Albert Orsborn[20]

No Room

••

*'She gave birth to her firstborn, a son. She wrapped him in
cloths and placed him in a manger, because there was no room
for them in the inn' (v. 7).*

No Nativity play is complete without the innkeeper's traditional one-liner: 'There is no room in the inn.' But the fact is that the inn-keeper went on to find room – of a sort – and so played a vital role in God's earth-changing incarnation plan. Today, millions still shut God out. But – daily, one by one – individuals who allow him a toehold in their lives find their lives transformed by the teaching and the presence of that Christ-child who uttered his first cry in a humble stable.

Bethlehem

I saw three wise-guys
Yesterday
In Bethlehem.
I couldn't reach
Your 'birthplace'
For their postcards
And their junk
And camels to be photographed.
Lord, how the tourists
Groaned and laughed,
And how the gutters stunk!

A hundred wooden babies
In a hundred wooden mangers
Were going cheap
At half the price
To half a hundred strangers.

I couldn't but be cynical
However much I tried,
Till faint among the souvenirs
I thought a Baby cried?

Mary's Treasured Memories

....

*'All who heard it were amazed at what the shepherds said
to them. But Mary treasured up all these things and pondered
them in her heart' (v. 18).*

Much can be said about Mary, though most of it is speculation. We can only imagine her reaction at various incidents – the initial news from the angel, the boy Jesus' intellectual conversations with teachers of the law, the miracles he performed, his death on the cross. Mary kept no diary. Apart from her 'songs' (which, admittedly, are very revealing) there is no written record of her thoughts. But we do know that she had them. Luke tells us she 'treasured up all these things and pondered them in her heart'.

Certainly, Mary was not a typical first-century Palestinian woman. It's no exaggeration to describe her circumstances as unique in the history of the world. And she was absolutely right when she declared: 'From now on all generations will call me blessed' (v. 48).

Mary had much to ponder, from the prophecies about her son to his final words before ascending to heaven. We know she reached an early decision to trust him – at the wedding feast when the wine ran out she told the servants to do whatever Jesus said (John 2:5), even though she had no inkling what would result. Some of the things he said must have hurt her – such as his declaration that he had no family but God (Matthew 12:48–50).

I take heart, though, that the Bible tells us Mary 'treasured' her thoughts. Throughout it all – even her deep grief at Calvary – she clearly had an inner peace of the sort we are told 'transcends human understanding'. The promise of God to each of us is that we too can know such peace.

....

Peace, perfect peace, far beyond all understanding;
Peace, perfect peace, left with us by Christ, our Lord.
Peace, perfect peace, through eternities expanding;
Peace, perfect peace! Peace, perfect peace!

Erik Leidzén[21]

Wise Men

∙∙

'Magi from the east came to Jerusalem and asked, "Where is the one who has been born king of the Jews? We saw his star in the east and have come to worship him"' (vv. 1, 2).

The Magi were probably astrologers from Persia or Arabia who were convinced that a new star that had appeared in the sky would lead them to a newborn child of royal roots. As such they would be well educated and wealthy. We don't know how many of them there were (merely that they brought with them three gifts) but it would have been very unwise to travel on such a journey without protection, and they probably had servants with them as well as armed guards. So their party was probably much larger than the three men on camels pictured on millions of Christmas cards.

Sadly (in romantic terms) the stable pictured on the cards is probably incorrect too. It is likely that the Magi did not arrive until some time after the birth of Jesus, by which time Mary and Joseph had surely moved on to better accommodation. Scripture records: 'On coming to the house, they saw the child with his mother Mary, and they bowed down and worshipped him' (v. 11).

King Herod, from whom the Magi asked guidance, was not really king of the Jews. He was not a Jew at all but was appointed king of Judea by the Roman Senate. The Jews neither respected nor loved him. And his act of slaughtering all the boys in Bethlehem under the age of two caused them to hate him all the more. Bethlehem was only a large village, so the number of children killed was probably smaller than many might think, but it was still a most dreadful act of state terrorism. For it to be linked to the birth of the Prince of Peace is a terrible blasphemy as well as an act of outrageous barbarism.

In this Christmas season, as millions put world peace on their 'virtual wish list', let's remember that peace begins with individuals. Each of us has a part to play.

∙∙

To pray:
'Lord, make me an instrument of thy peace.'

Francis of Assisi

One of his Greatest Gifts

....

*'If you really knew me, you would know my Father as well.
From now on, you do know him and have seen him . . . Anyone
who has seen me has seen the Father' (vv. 7, 9).*

On this Christmas Eve, let's stand back from the traditional Nativity story and consider one of the greatest gifts God gives to each of us. It comes wrapped in a short sentence from Matthew's Gospel: 'Surely I am with you always, to the very end of the age' (28:20). The presence of Christ in our lives is a priceless gift.

And let's think deeply, too, of the truth found in today's reading: 'Anyone who has seen me has seen the Father' (v. 9). On the first Christmas Eve no one had seen God in the way it became possible to see him after the birth of Jesus the next day. For the next thirty years a small number of people were able to see him in the flesh, but perhaps more important is the fact that all Christians now have the opportunity to see the true nature of God in the person of Christ, as recorded in God's Word.

'Like father, like son' is not universally true, which is not always bad. Some fathers provide a less-than-perfect example for their children. But in the case of the Father–Son relationship within the Trinity, we have it confirmed from Jesus himself that he and the Father are one. So when we see the love which characterises Jesus' nature we see the love that is God, for God is love.

Some Christians believe there is one Christmas carol, written by John Byrom, that should really be saved for Christmas Day. Certainly the first two lines will have special relevance tomorrow:

> Christians awake, salute the happy morn
> Whereon the Saviour of the world was born!

But let me remind you of the important words of the third verse, which remind us of the consequences of God's love for us:

> O may we keep and ponder in our mind
> God's wondrous love in saving lost mankind.
> Trace we the babe, who hath retrieved our loss,
> From his poor manger to his bitter cross;
> Tread in his steps, assisted by his grace,
> Till man's first heavenly state again takes place.

Good tidings of great joy!

Recognition

'My eyes have seen your salvation' (v. 30).

If we have the opportunity on this Christmas Day to share in worship with others we may well be encouraged to sing the carol which is particularly relevant to this day: 'A child this day is born, a child of high renown.' In the last verse we will have the chance to raise our voices joyfully and sing: 'All glory be to God who reigns enthroned on high.' Our singing will confirm that we have recognised the identity of that child and wish to declare our acceptance of his sovereignty over us.

If we followed the Christmas story chronologically, it would be a few days before we considered the story of Simeon, who is the subject of the reading I have chosen for today. But I feel it right, on this Christmas Day, to remind ourselves – through Simeon – that Christ's coming was in answer to a promise of God.

Says Simeon: 'I have seen your salvation which you have made ready for every people' (vv. 30, 31, *JBP*).

As we celebrate this very special day, let none of us fail to recognise the identity of the one whose birthday we honour. Let's acknowledge him as the source of our personal salvation, as well as the salvation of the world.

> All our hearts rejoice this morning,
> On this happy Christmas day;
> Praise and joy to God we're sounding,
> Love and peace have come our way.
> Jesus Christ, our loving Saviour,
> Came to earth with gifts sublime;
> Let us join our voices singing;
> What a glory, he is mine!
>
> His salvation freely given
> Is his gift to all mankind . . .
> *Ernest Henry Parr*

Of all the gifts we unwrap today, none will match God's gift to us of his Son, the world's Saviour . . . and mine . . . and yours!

Christmas Gifts for Christ?

....

'I was hungry and you gave me something to eat, I was thirsty and you gave me something to drink, I was a stranger and you invited me in, I needed clothes and you clothed me, I was sick and you looked after me, I was in prison and you came to visit me' (vv. 35, 36).

Are you surprised at the reading I have suggested for Boxing Day? Look again at verse 40: 'Whatever you did for one of the least of these brothers of mine, you did for me.' Most of us will have given presents to others this Christmas. But how many of us gave gifts to people we do not care about?

We happily give to our family, our friends and perhaps people we have a measure of responsibility for – a manager might customarily give small gifts to members of his team, for example . . . almost out of a sense of duty. If only everyone saw themselves as having responsibility for everyone else! And if only we gave all our gifts out of love for them! It would be a different world, a better world.

But, you say, you cannot give gifts to six billion people. Of course you can't! Not gifts in the sense of material things wrapped in pretty paper and tied with ribbon. But our gift to the world can be the way we live.

This Boxing Day each of us can resolve, perhaps, 'to live more simply, so that others may simply live'. We can decide to have nothing to do with commercial practices that treat some people unjustly. We can embrace fair trade when we shop. We can raise our voice when inequality comes to our attention. We can choose not to read publications which degrade women, and not to vote for political parties which urge discrimination against ethnic minorities.

When we do so, for the sake of the deprived and dispossessed, we do it for Christ – who is incarnate in those people, as he is in us.

What do we have that we can give to others? A compassionate heart, perhaps? A listening ear? The experience of the years, expressed in wise counselling, offered not condescendingly but as friend to friend? When we give these things to others, we give them to the Christ-child who became our Lord. Those are the gifts he wants from us.

Everything

••

'When Joseph and Mary had done everything required by the Law of the Lord, they returned to Galilee to their own town of Nazareth' (v. 39).

Scripture tells us that after the birth of Jesus his earthly parents were meticulous in following the requirements of the Jewish faith. Jesus was circumcised on the eighth day and at the appropriate time Mary and Joseph travelled to Jerusalem 'to present him to the Lord' in the temple, a ceremony required of every family's firstborn male, and to offer the specified sacrifice of 'a pair of doves or two young pigeons'.

The occasion was made particularly memorable for Mary and Joseph by the reaction of two observers – Simeon and Anna. Simeon recognised the baby Jesus as 'the Lord's Christ', and spoke words which his parents clearly never forgot, and Anna – a respected prophetess – 'spoke about the child to all who were looking forward to the redemption of Jerusalem' (v. 38). And then Scripture tells us: 'When Joseph and Mary had done everything required by the Law of the Lord, they returned to Galilee to their own town of Nazareth.'

There is something reassuringly complete about that word 'everything'. Having done everything we can, or everything we must, we should in theory have no fear or guilt that we have acted inadequately or irresponsibly. If we have met all the requirements, we have done our duty. But there is no suggestion here that Mary and Joseph acted merely out of a sense of duty. Rather, Scripture suggests they were people of devout faith. They did what was required out of a deep sense of commitment to God, and gratitude to him.

And so it should be for us. A sense of duty is an honourable quality, but the best motivation is gratitude and love. In these post-Christmas days, let's not lose too quickly the sense of awe that comes to us when we ponder the amazing truth that God should willingly leave the glory of heaven to live among us on earth, simply because he loves us. Hymn-writer Isaac Watts declared:

> Love so amazing, so divine,
> Demands my soul, my life, my all.

There we have it – my all. Everything!

Quieten Down

....

'Be still, and know that I am God' (v. 10).

In some countries of the world, Christmas Day is the only oasis of calm in a hectic, non-stop year, with shopping centres and travel systems closing down for a unique twenty-four hours of inactivity. But those hours soon pass, and life quickly returns to the 'normal' state of incessant busyness and noise. And so it is, too, in our relationships – more talking than listening, more handing-out of sometimes glib 'solutions' than simple sharing of painful experiences. 'Be still,' says God. But sometimes we are too busy to hear him.

Chatter

I talk too much!
Incessantly I chatter
Of many things
That really
Just don't matter.
When people come
Intent to bare their hearts,
It's then this wild impulse
To chatter starts.
I reel out remedies
Before I know
The depth of their despair,
Their width of woe.
And breathlessly
I have my silly say,
Till, with a sigh,
They simply go away!

O help me, Lord,
To play the listener's part,
To seal my lips
And open wide my heart!

Reconciliation

'We come therefore as Christ's ambassadors. It is as if God were appealing to you through us: in Christ's name, we implore you, be reconciled to God!' (v. 20, NEB).

Christmas is a great time for family get-togethers. But, sadly, the brotherly and sisterly love on display at reunions sometimes doesn't survive more than a day or two. Three or four days later – by 29 December, say! – the atmosphere can be a bit fraught as the Monopoly board is produced for the umpteenth time. By then, perhaps, reconciliation should be the name of the game.

These days, the word 'reconciliation' is mostly used in connection with industrial tribunals, or negotiations between employers and unions over disputes, or as part of the discussions warring marriage partners engage in prior to taking the final steps towards divorce. Reconciliation in such circumstances is much to be desired.

In fact, reconciliation is never a bad thing. It's a silver lining without a cloud.

It's always good for people to 'make up' after a disagreement (the kissing is optional!) and in today's reading Paul tells us the most important reconciliation we should aim for, when it is needed, is between us and God. The glorious news is that Christ makes such reconciliation possible: 'From first to last this has been the work of God. He has reconciled us men to himself through Christ, and he has enlisted us in this service of reconciliation. What I mean is, that God was in Christ reconciling the world to himself, no longer holding men's misdeeds against them' (18, 19, *NEB*).

As this year ends, let's examine our relationship with God, and see if anything has come between us, spoiling the beautiful friendship that is God's plan for each of us. If reconciliation is needed, let's make the prayer we need to make, knowing it will be joyfully answered.

Knowing my failings, knowing my fears,
Seeing my sorrows, drying my tears,
Jesus recall me, me re-ordain;
You know I love you, use me again.

J. G.

Attitude

••

'Your attitude should be the same as that of Christ Jesus: Who,
being in very nature God, did not consider equality with God
something to be grasped, but made himself nothing,
taking the very nature of a servant' (vv. 5–7).

As I come to the end of my time as writer of *Words of Life* (just tomorrow to go!) may I share something of my testimony with you, relating it to some of the things Paul talks about in today's reading? Let me question myself, and share my answers with you.

Do you receive encouragement from being united with Christ? Yes. I have always felt that Christ understands me and wants me to develop spiritually. He is an unfailing encourager!

Have you received comfort from Christ's love? Even when I have made mistakes of which I am ashamed, I have felt his love and known his forgiveness. Our God has a gift for forgetting!

Do you enjoy personal fellowship with the Spirit? Yes. Even when I have been tempted to abandon my faith in him, he has hung on to me. Paul reminds me: 'If a man does not possess the Spirit of Christ, he is no Christian' (Romans 8:9, *NEB*). I daily claim the fellowship of that Spirit.

Does your God express any tenderness and compassion? He *is* tenderness. He *is* compassion. He *is* love! These are constantly offered to me, even when I don't really deserve them.

Do you have ambitions for the future? Oh yes! And in today's Bible verses Paul tells me what some of them should be. I should aim to be of a like mind to Jesus, sharing his purposes and affections, devoid of vain conceit and selfishness, looking to the interests of others, having the nature of a servant and – summing everything up – the attitude of Christ.

My highest hope? It is that people will see something of Christ in me in the moments when I am unaware that I am being observed. If I look like Christ only when I am trying desperately to give the appearance of being his keenest follower, then I probably know little of him. Having the same attitude as Christ is not a part-time option. It's all or nothing, always or never. My aim is all, always.

Greater Things

••

'I tell you the truth, anyone who has faith in me will do what I have been doing. He will do even greater things than these' (v. 12).

It saddens me, around this time every year, how quickly the Christmas spirit wears off among those people who wear their Christian faith lightly – putting it on like a rarely worn overcoat for their annual visit to church for a carol service. Just a few days later, the seasonal cut-price sales in the shops occupy their minds, plus, of course, tonight's New Year's Eve parties. It's a shame. Christmas isn't just for Christmas! But, fair enough – the old year ends today, and a new one begins tomorrow. And here's a suggestion from me: how about dubbing 2009 'The Year of Greater Things'? I have in mind the words of Jesus: 'The person who trusts me will not only do what I'm doing but even greater things' (v. 12, *MSG*).

Greater things than Jesus did? Oh, my! Surely not! Water into wine, five thousand people fed with a few bread rolls, dead men raised to life – how can any of us perform miracles remotely like that, let alone greater? Well, perhaps those are not the sort of things the Lord needs from us. Perhaps he wants less spectacular, but no less important, things.

Having said that, any preacher who today is granted a few minutes' air-time on national radio or television, addressing an audience of millions, has the opportunity to tell the gospel message to more people than Jesus ever did. Greater things? It's possible.

In today's reading, Philip says to Jesus, 'Lord, show us the Father and that will be enough for us' (v. 8). Jesus' reply reveals a momentary sadness – or could it be frustration? 'Don't you know me, Philip, even after I have been among you such a long time?' Then he continues: 'Anyone who has seen me has seen the Father.' How I wish all those nominal Christians who have gazed into the manger this Christmas for a glimpse of the Christ-child would realise this truth!

Jesus then offers his miracles as evidence of his divine identity. But goes on to tell his disciples that they, too, can do what he has done. It's an amazing truth to take into the new year. In the words of a former world leader of The Salvation Army, General Albert Orsborn: 'Give us faith, O Lord, we pray, faith for greater things.'

Notes

1 Lucy Milward Booth-Hellberg, 'Keep On Believing' in *The Musical Salvationist* (January 1889), © Salvationist Publishing & Supplies Ltd.

2 Richard Slater, 'Never Mind: Go On!' in *The Musical Salvationist* (December 1886), © Salvationist Publishing & Supplies Ltd.

3 Colin Fairclough, 'Christ of Glory, Prince of Peace', Song 479 in *The Song Book of The Salvation Army*, © 1986 The General of The Salvation Army.

4 Quoted in Klyne Snodgrass, *The NIV Application Commentary: Ephesians*, © 1996 Zondervan.

5 Francis Foulkes, *Tyndale New Testament Commentaries – Ephesians*, © 2007 IVP.

6 William Barclay, *The Daily Study Bible*, © 2002 St Andrew Press.

7 Quoted in Klyne Snodgrass, *The NIV Application Commentary: Ephesians*, © 1996 Zondervan.

8 Ibid.

9 Ibid.

10 *Great Quotes and Illustrations*, compiled by George Sweeting, © 1990 Word Publishing.

11 Ibid.

12 Ibid.

13 Frances Wilkinson, *Growing Up in Christ*, © 1960 SCM Press.

14 Grace Stuart, *Private World of Pain*, © 1953 George Allen & Unwin.

15 Revd Leslie J. Tizard, *Facing Life and Death*, © 1959 George Allen & Unwin.

16 Joy Davidman, *Smoke on the Mountain: An Interpretation of the Ten Commandments*, © 1954 The Westminster Press.

17 Corrie ten Boom, *The Hiding Place*, © 2004 Hodder & Stoughton.

18 Viktor E. Frankl, *The Unconscious God*, © 1977 Hodder & Stoughton.

19 Paul Tournier, *Guilt and Grace*, © 1962 HarperCollins Publishers.

20 Albert Orsborn, 'Shepherd, Hear My Prayer' in *The Musical Salvationist* (July/August 1946), © Salvationist Publishing & Supplies Ltd.

21 Erik Leidzén, 'Peace, Perfect Peace', Song 751 in *The Song Book of The Salvation Army*, © 1986 The General of The Salvation Army.

INDEX
September–December 2008
(as from May–August 2003)

Subscribe...

Words of Life is published three times a year:
January-April, May-August and September-December.

Four easy ways to subscribe
- By post – simply complete and return the subscription form below
- By phone – +44 (0)1933 445 445
- By email – mail_order@sp-s.co.uk
- Or pop into your local Christian bookshop

SUBSCRIPTION FORM

Name (Miss, Mrs, Ms, Mr) ....

Address ....

....

.... Postcode ....

Tel. No. ....

Email* ....

Annual Subscription Rates
UK **£10.50** *Non-UK* £10.50 + £3.90 P&P = **£14.40**

Please send me .... copy/copies of the next three issues of *Words of Life*
commencing with **January 2009**

Total: £ .... **I enclose payment by cheque** ☐
Please make cheques payable to *The Salvation Army*

Please debit my Access/Mastercard/Visa/American Express/Switch card

Card No. ☐☐☐☐ ☐☐☐☐ ☐☐☐☐ ☐☐☐☐   **Expiry date:** ___ /___

Security No. ☐☐☐ **Issue number (Switch only)** _____

Cardholder's signature: .... **Date:** ....

Please send this form and any cheques to: **The Mail Order Department,
Salvationist Publishing and Supplies, 66–78 Denington Road, Denington
Industrial Estate, Wellingborough, Northamptonshire NN8 2QH, UK**

☐ *We would like to keep in touch with you by placing you on our mailing list. If
you would prefer not to receive correspondence from us, please tick this box. The
Salvation Army does not sell or lease its mailing lists.